Contractarianism versus Holism

Reinterpreting Locke's

Two Treatises of Government

Zbigniew Rau

University Press of America, Inc.
Lanham • New York • London

Copyright © 1995 by
University Press of America,® Inc.
4720 Boston Way
Lanham, Maryland 20706

3 Henrietta Street
London, WC2E 8LU England

All rights reserved
Printed in the United States of America
British Cataloging in Publication Information Available

Library of Congress Cataloging-in-Publication Data

Rau, Zbigniew
Contractarianism versus holism : reinterpreting Locke's Two treatises of government / Zbigniew Rau.
p. cm.
Includes index.
1. Locke, John, 1632-1704. Two treatises of government. 2. Locke, John, 1632-1704—Contributions in political science. 3. Filmer, Robert, Sir, d. 1653—Contributions in political science. I. Title.
JC153.L83R38   1995   320'.01'1--dc20   95-6234 CIP

ISBN 0-8191-9929-X (cloth: alk: paper)
ISBN 0-8191-9930-3 (pbk: alk: paper)

∞™ The paper used in this publication meets the minimum requirements of American National Standard for Information Sciences—Permanence of Paper for Printed Library Materials,

Contents

Preface	vi
Acknowledgments	vii
Introduction	1
The Controversy	5
I. Scholarly efforts to define Filmerism	5
II. Main features of Filmer's and Locke's systems	9
III. Redefining Filmer and Locke	10
The State of Nature	25
Power and Property	43
The Principles of Civil Society	67
I. The individual as the only source of political power	70
II. Political power is limited	73
III. Consent of individuals as only criterion of legitimacy of political power	80
IV. The voluntary character of adherence to the political structure	89
The Position and Structure of Civil Government	105
The Concept of Resistance	123
Conclusion	143
Index	147

Preface

This book is intended to offer a concise, comprehensive reinterpretation of John Locke's political thought as stated in his *Two Treatises of Government*. Though this reinterpretation is deeply rooted in the classical liberal tradition, it does cast the enterprise in the theoretically significant terms of a central conflict in contemporary social and political theory, thus linking it directly to the political problems and ideological dilemmas of a late twentieth century audience.

I have structured the book to make it maximally accessible. The introduction and conclusion define the parameters and implications of the book's argument, and link Locke's thought directly to contemporary ideological and political debates. Each chapter begins with opening remarks that let the reader know where he is in the broader argument. The narrative itself focuses almost without interruption on its central task, that is, on moving the conceptual argument forward; those points that are of scholarly or incidental interest are discussed more thoroughly in the footnotes.

The book does not presume a prior knowledge of the main currents of Locke studies and is thus accessible to upper-level undergraduate or graduate students of Locke, political theory, or the history of political ideas. It purposefully avoids a conventional analysis of the historical background of Locke's thought and the internal disputes of contemporary Locke scholarship. The reader is instead offered original research, a new perspective, fresh insights, and, in the chapter summaries and footnotes, comparisons with the claims of most other scholars in the last decades of Locke studies.

Acknowledgments

This book would not have been possible without the encouragement and support of various people and institutions to whom I would like to express my gratitude.

My greatest debt goes to Peter Laslett. He invited me to England, where this and other Locke projects I had worked on could develop and improve. He was a constant and unfailing source of intellectual inspiration and stimulation. It was in our long and regular conversations on Filmer and Locke that my idea for this book was finally shaped.

My discussions with John Dunn helped clarify the opposition between holism and contractarianism. In conversations with Quentin Skinner and Gordon Schochet I managed to better understand the concepts of the state of nature, society, and civil society in Locke. Philip Pettit was kind enough to provide me with extensive written comments concerning the theoretical setting of the book as expressed in chapter one.

I wish to express my appreciation to the Master and Fellows of Trinity College, Cambridge for their generous support of my work and for appointing me a Visiting Fellow Commoner in 1985-88. The final completion of the book was possible due to the support of the Research School of Social Sciences, Australian National University, where I spent a semester in 1993 as a Visiting Fellow.

My very personal thanks go to Jamila Abdelghani for her very important comments concerning the final structure of the book and for providing extensive editorial assistance.

Introduction

There is a powerful tendency among most prominent Locke scholars to argue that the key to understanding John Locke's doctrine is to be found in the historical context from which it originated, that is, in the political conflicts and philosophical conceptions of the seventeenth century. Thus, he is presented by Peter Laslett as an intellectual supporter of the political struggle of his protector, Earl Shaftesbury; he is portrayed by John Dunn as a theologically minded Protestant philosopher of his own time; he is described by James Tully as a Thomist thinker engaged in the property rights debate with his contemporary natural law theorists; and he is characterized by Richard Ashcraft as a radical ideologue of the first mass political movement in his country.[1]

Without disputing the merits of these interpretations, in this book I take a very different approach. Attempting to recast contemporary understanding of Locke's political doctrine, I examine its conceptual dimension in relation to the alternative doctrine of his opponent, Robert Filmer. That Locke deliberately and purposefully concentrated on this dimension in his *Two Treatises of Government* becomes clear when adequate attention is paid to the rest of this work's title: *In the Former, The False Principles and Foundation of Sir Robert Filmer, And His Followers, are Detected and Overthrown. The Latter is an*

Essay concerning The True Original, Extent, and End of Civil-Government. In fact, he was directing his argument against his adversary's major discourse, *Patriarcha: A Defence of the Natural Power of Kings against the Unnatural Liberty of the People*, intending to invalidate its principles and provide a legitimate alternative. Thus, to reduce Locke's thought either to his place in history in isolation from Filmer or, alternatively, to his stand on issues such as property, consent, or rights, as do most political theorists, misses much of the point. Considering the whole body of the controversy remedies this insufficiency. What emerges when Locke's thought is explored in relation to that of Filmer's is the coherence of each of their systems and the manner in which their controversy transcends its antiquarian appeal and echoes contemporary debates in social and political theory. Accordingly, the framework of this book's discussion is the controversy in social and political theory between individualism-cum-contractarianism and metaphysical holism.

Taking both thinkers as systematic philosophers, I begin my analysis with two basic claims. In chapter one I argue that first, the essence of Filmer's system is not patriarchalism—as is commonly assumed in scholarship—but holism. Second, by illustrating the difference between methodological individualism—which is commonly treated as the opposite of holism—and contractarianism, I show that Locke, in looking for a comprehensive argument against holism, had to construct the contractarian model; individualism alone would not do. Very different systems then emerge from Filmer's and Locke's opposing premises. The myriad levels upon which the clash of these systems is expressed are examined by providing detailed discussions of their positions on such issues as property, civil society, consent, legitimacy, government, and resistance.

Although the language and particular examples that Filmer and Locke use seem archaic, the principles which underlie and resonate throughout their systems reflect two timeless, opposing visions of social and political relations. Indeed, if the antiquated particulars are ignored, the very familiar and contemporary debate over the interaction between individuals, society, and the state emerges. One system offers the notion of deterministic, metaphysical forces leading the social and political process. The other conceives the free individual agent as capable of constructing politics according to his own will. One considers the social and political context natural. The other treats it as man-made. One sees the social and political whole as the primary category of political thinking. The other points to the individual as that category. One believes that the individual derives the essence and meaning of his existence from the social and political context. The other argues that it is the individual that gives the essence and meaning to this context. One considers property dependent on and the result of the social and political context. The other treats it as dependent on and the result of an individual's effort. One claims that politics is conformed to the rights, interests, and needs of the social and political whole. The other maintains that politics is determined by the rights, interests, and needs of the individual. One asserts that the social and political order expresses the standards of rationality of the social whole. The other says that this order is based on the individual's standards of rationality. One conceptually conforms the individual to society and society to the state. The other defends the conceptual priority of the individual over society and that of society over the state. One claims that rulers make themselves legitimate by virtue of exercising their power. The other insists that the legitimacy of government is based on the consent of individuals united in society. One maintains that political obligation is unconditional and rejects the notion of resistance. The other stresses that this obligation has a conditional character and considers resistance legitimate.

Like the contemporaries of Filmer and Locke, we have yet to finally commit ourselves to one set of these propositions over the other. We have not even agreed on the final composition of each set. The argument continues, in classrooms, print, policy making—and in embattled regions—between the supporters of one model, holism (most commonly found in contemporary Marxism, communitarianism, nationalism, and religious fundamentalism) and the other, contractarianism (present in today's varieties of liberalism). Thus, the dilemmas which Filmer and Locke address remain as much ours as theirs. But in their case, because each believed in the urgency of his polemic, seeing it as an opportunity to offer an alternative solution to the political conflicts that were tearing apart their country, they honed their arguments into sharp, powerful systems in the hope that their philosophical consistency would be translated into politically efficient constitutional blueprints. As a result, their debate enables us to see the depth of the opposition between holism and contractarianism, one that rings with great clarity and provides a clear statement of political and philosophical alternatives. In light of this, reducing Locke's thought to intellectual history or to fragmented concepts of political theory would be inexcusably simplistic—not only would it impoverish our understanding of their controversy—it would deny us a look at ourselves in a seventeenth century mirror.

---

[1] Peter Laslett, "Introduction" in John Locke, *Two Treatises of Government*, Peter Laslett, ed. (Cambridge: Cambridge University Press, 1960); John Dunn, *The Political Thought of John Locke* (Cambridge: Cambridge University Press, 1969); James Tully, *A Discourse on Property: John Locke and his Adversaries* (Cambridge: Cambridge University Press, 1980); Richard Ashcraft, *Revolutionary Politics and Locke's Two Treatises of Government* (Princeton: Princeton University Press, 1986).

Chapter 1

The Controversy

My purpose in this chapter is to present the conceptual dimension of the controversy between Filmer and Locke. I shall set forth the claim that the essence of Filmer's system is not patriarchalism, as is generally supposed, but holism. In defending this claim, I shall show that Filmer's argument is incoherent when seen through the lens of patriarchalism and that this incoherence disappears and the argument falls into place when defined as holistic. I shall then argue that Locke's contractarianism (and not methodological individualism, which is commonly considered the opposite to holism) is the appropriate counterpart of holism—and that the opposition between contractarianism and holism is central not only to this particular controversy between Filmer and Locke, but to the history of political thought as a whole. What the controversy between Filmer and Locke offers is a unique view of the clash between holism and contractarianism: it is one in which the two parties could not be more fundamentally opposed, and which, in taking the form of direct polemic, produces a sharpness and clarity that strips the arguments to their most fundamental claims.

Scholarly efforts to define Filmerism

Since the publication of Peter Laslett's works on Locke and Filmer,[1] two propositions have been commonly accepted in scholarship. The first is that Filmer was not simply Locke's whipping boy, his opportunity to attack Hobbes by proxy, but rather a political thinker in his own right, and the author of a highly original system of political thought—not simply a generic advocate of absolutism. The second proposition is that it was Filmer—as the author of a previous system—that set the terms of Locke's argument. The direction of the development of Locke's system indicates his intention to refute particular segments of Filmer's theory. Therefore, based on these propositions, it can be assumed that Filmer's *Patriarcha* and Locke's *Two Treatises* offer opposing explanations of fundamental questions in political philosophy at the same conceptual level (or, at least, at similar levels). The particular framework of each system, however, remains to be defined. To do this, one must define Filmer's system and then characterize Locke's system as its conceptual opposite.

Orthodox scholarship claims that the essence of the Filmerian system is patriarchalism. In his pioneering book on patriarchalism, Gordon Schochet writes:

> In essence, Filmer's thought was a defense of divine right absolutism on the ground that the political order in Stuart England had evolved from the family, magistrates were therefore entitled to the same filial obedience that children owed their fathers.[2]

This claim is supported not only by textual evidence but also by consideration of the social and intellectual environment which shaped Filmer's system. Contemporary scholarship indicates that in Filmer's time patriarchalism was a well-established doctrine. Schochet stresses that various elements of patriarchalism were already present in the main body of pre-Filmerian Western and English political thought.[3] Laslett points out that the everyday experience of the seventeenth century Englishman confirmed patriarchalist assumptions. This experience was by no means limited to his private family life: it also extended to the public sphere, since the social structure of the country—and indeed the political system itself—was often conceived in patriarchalist terms. To take a single example, it was on the basis of the fifth commandment's demand of obedience to paternal authority that the teaching of the Church of England commonly demanded obedience to both family and political authority.[4] Moreover, J.C.D. Clark maintains that English society's patriarchalist attitude was independent of the particular political figures ruling at the central government level; as a result, it lasted even into the nineteenth century.[5] Therefore, it is argued, the patriarchalist essence of Filmer's system was not so much the product of the intellectual reflection of its author as it was an accumulation of patriarchalist assumptions Filmer drew from the outside world. Without disputing this analysis of the influence of Filmer's social and intellectual environment, it is worth considering whether patriarchalism, as the alleged essence of his system, actually is the fundamental alternative to Locke's system. Schochet insists that in seventeenth century English political thought the alternative to patriarchalism was contractarianism. Accordingly, he claims, the controversy between Filmer and Locke took place along this line. Yet even following Schochet's account, it is difficult to see the debate between patriarchalism and contractarianism as one that concerned fundamental issues. Schochet himself indicates that in many respects, patriarchalism is reconcilable with contractarianism. Indeed, he suggests that some elements of patriarchalism can be found in Hobbes and Locke, even though at the time they were writing, contractarian concepts were not commonly thought to explain the source of political obligation, but were instead used to explain how people entered into given social structures.[6] Therefore, the characterization of the controversy between Filmer and Locke as one between patriarchalism and contractarianism does not fully take into account the controversy's conceptual dimension.

More importantly, it is worth asking whether patriarchalism provides a suitable basis for the various elements of Filmer's own argument. If one takes patriarchalism to be the essence of Filmer's system, it becomes difficult to define the framework of that system. This point has been addressed by scholars and is usually connected with two observations. First, Filmer did make use of the main canons of patriarchalism, but patriarchalism did not define the shape of his doctrine. Second, the fundamental concept of Filmer's system, that is, the concept of power, undermines the main canons of patriarchalism. R.W.K. Hinton, who takes this position, calls Filmer a "unique patriarchalist," and states that "his most emphatic statement on the subject of fathers is simply that subordination of children is the fountain of all regal authority." Hinton goes on to point out that Filmer,

> could not magnify fathers without diminishing kings, his kings could not be sovereign without making fathers impotent... Filmer's ultimate statement on fathers and rulers—though he did not make it [explicitly]—was that between a great gulf was fixed. Rulers were sovereign, fathers nothing: rulers had all power, fathers had none. Surely in a sense this is the negation of patriarchalism. At all events by conventional standards it was a very eccentric form of it.[7]

In other words, for Filmer the dominant force is that of sovereign power and not that of the family in any form. Accordingly, it is the concept of sovereignty and not patriarchalism that determines the character of Filmer's system. James Daly takes this thought a step further:

> At the heart [of Filmer's thought] was the concept of omnicompetent sovereignty, sovereignty unrestricted, unlimited, unbounded, from which there was no appeal and within which there was a radical simplicity.... This sovereignty was the only political binding force that could exist, or ever had existed.[8]

And therefore,

> one is even tempted to relegate patriarchalism in Filmer to the status of necessary hypothesis, a *deus ex machina*, indispensable to start the argument off, but relatively unimportant in its elaboration.[9]

Yet, if one's aim is to grasp the full conceptual dimension of the controversy between Filmer and Locke, understanding sovereignty as the essence of Filmerism proves no more useful than the similar understanding of patriarchalism. Supporting this point are Daly's attempts to classify Filmer's system: "Filmerism's core lay in the doctrine of sovereignty. In that doctrine Filmer most resembled Hobbes."[10] Following Daly's conclusion, one could assume that if Filmer championed sovereignty the same way Hobbes did, then the argument of the *Two Treatises* could be aimed against *Leviathan* in the same way it was against *Patriarcha*. Yet such an interpretation cannot be easily defended in light of Laslett's compelling analysis of the contextual, textual, and conceptual evidence, which points to Filmer, not Hobbes, as Locke's target.[11] Moreover, had Filmer's system been based on the Hobbesian concept of sovereignty, Locke's dispute with him would have focused more on constitutional considerations concerning the structure of the state and the extent of the power of the magistrate. Indeed, if this had been the case, the controversy would have taken a different shape since—despite serious philosophical differences between Locke and Hobbes—it would have revolved more around disagreement over political issues rather than disagreement over philosophical premises.[12]

The point is, then, that the key to Filmer's system is philosophical, not political. As W. H. Greenleaf points out, "the basis of Filmer's political thought may be seen fundamentally as a version of the political theory of order. No analysis of his ideas which neglects this aspect—which is philosophical, rather than scriptural, historical or legal—can be adequate."[13] Such a reading of Filmerism might make it easier to understand why the controversy between Filmer and Locke reached down to the very fundamentals of political philosophy. Nevertheless, Greenleaf himself neither presses this point further nor explores the philosophical character of Filmer's argument.

It is now possible to sum up the efforts by scholars to define Filmerism. First, Filmer drew upon the main body of patriarchalist concepts, but patriarchalism did not itself constitute the essence of his system. Second, the dominant notion of his doctrine was that of sovereign power, since it shaped the very framework of the system. Third, sovereign power in Filmer was not a political but a philosophical concept.

The main features of Filmer's and Locke's systems

At the bottom of Filmer's system lies the ontological assumption that a superhuman agency is the key to understanding social relations.[14] This agency is paternal power. Paternal power is chronologically and conceptually prior to mankind and therefore to all human relations and all institutions of private and public life. Paternal power is governed by macroscopic laws which are *sui generis* and which state that the power is both temporally and spatially immanent. On the one hand, the existence of paternal power is infinite or, failing that, it will last as long as mankind itself. On the other hand, paternal power serves as the factor which unifies all human beings. Indeed, the pattern of paternal power is followed in all human bonds, private and public. No human relations exist outside of paternal power, since it has no external boundary.

Given the chronological and conceptual priority of paternal power with respect to mankind, individuals exist for the sake of that power; it does not exist for the sake of individuals. Human beings are the medium through which properties of paternal power are manifested. In Filmer, individuals are divided into two categories, distinguished by their relation to that power: the rulers, who exercise it, and their subjects, over whom it is exercised. Indeed, the relation to paternal power is the only aspect of human life Filmer is interested in. His whole concept of human nature is deduced from the properties of paternal power, and reduced to the function individuals perform in relations created by that power. People's desires and goals, as well as their capacity to realize them, result from these relations. The main characteristic of rulers is their ability to rule, and that of their subjects, to obey.

The conclusions that one can draw from the relation between paternal power and individuals in Filmer's system are straightforward. No human relation is man-made: all relations manifest some aspect of paternal power. In other words, paternal power is a given in every relation; its various forms remain essentially the same, simply reproducing themselves over generations. Under these circumstances, moral criticism of the existing state of affairs is impossible, since all standards are also given and also reproduce themselves. This renders all politics impotent.

In opposing this approach, Locke reversed all the premises of his adversary.[15] Contrary to Filmer, Locke's conceptual point of departure is the assumption that individual agents are the key to understanding social relations, and the only actual agents in the social process. Thus, the sum of individual lives make up the social context. Individuals are free agents who shape the social world according to their wills; civil society and civil government are their creation and act according to the standards they set up.

Given the chronological and conceptual priority of individuals with respect to all social institutions, Locke holds that such institutions exist for the sake of individuals, and not the other way around. The existence of any social relation or political institution depends upon the principles governing the human behavior of the individuals who have created them. Accordingly, the properties of social or political institutions are derived from a particular configuration of individuals—their dispositions, situations, beliefs, and physical resources—and the powers of these institutions are limited by the same factors. For example, the properties of civil government result from and are limited by the act of political trusteeship, in which the majority of civil society empowers the government with the promotion of the common good.

The conclusions Locke draws from the premises of his system are, accordingly, the opposite of Filmer's. If all social relations and political institutions are man-made, they cannot reproduce themselves. Rather, they can be reproduced only by their creators—individuals. But individuals can also change them in accordance with their preferences. Thus, whenever these relations and institutions cease to act according to the standards set up at the time of their establishment, individuals can undertake political action to reinforce these standards. Resistance to a government that has breached the trust of civil society is justified in this way.

Redefining Filmer and Locke

Using the output of the classical debate in social theory, it is possible to consider the opposing systems of Filmer and Locke as those of holism and methodological individualism. In fact, it is possible to argue that the main body of the opposition between them results from two fundamentally different approaches toward the issues of causality and reductionism in social relations.[16] Causality in holism is based upon the activity of a superhuman agency, while in methodological individualism it is based upon the activity of human agents. Holists reduce the properties of individuals to their functions in social wholes while individualists reduce the properties of social institutions to their functions in the service of the individuals who create them.

Accordingly, Filmer's system can be classified as holistic since its main features fully suit the methodological ideal type of holism. Filmer's paternal power, which cements all human relations, constitutes one social whole; it is thus a superhuman agency. This is the point of departure of any holistic causal explanation.[17] In turn, the properties of Filmer's individuals, that is, his rulers and the ruled, are functions of their place in that social whole; this is a notion that is a canon of holism.[18] Similarly, Locke's system can be classified as individualistic since its features are in basic agreement with the methodological ideal type of individualism. Locke's assumption that individual agents are the key to understanding social relations is the core of methodological individualism.[19] By the same token, Locke's claim that the properties of social or political institutions are derived from a particular configuration of individuals is also a standard part of the individualistic arsenal.[20]

Classifying the systems of Filmer and Locke as holistic and individualistic is plausible to the extent that it underscores the fundamental opposition between them as that opposition is expressed in the categories of social theory. However, although methodological individualism offers a fundamental alternative to holism, this alternative is not comprehensive. Indeed, the holistic model reaches much further than its individualistic counterpart. In the holistic model of social explanation, the content of each of its three elements is definitive: a superhuman agency that has its own standards of rationality (H^1), relations among individuals created and defined by the superhuman agency and reflecting its standards of rationality (H^2), and relations between these individuals and the superhuman agency created and defined by this agency and reflecting its standards of rationality (H^3). In the holistic model, the content of the second and third element follows from the content of the first element, that is, the presence of superhuman agency and its standards of rationality. In the individualistic model of social explanation, the content of only one element is definitive, namely that of human agency or the individuals themselves that have their own standards of rationality (I^1). The content of the two other elements, relations among the individuals (I^2) and relations between them and the social institutions created by them (I^3) are beyond the scope of the individualistic model.

Therefore, the individualistic explanatory model can be efficiently used only against $H,^1$ the first element of the holistic explanatory model. In fact, it is possible to argue that within the individualistic model individuals may create relations among themselves—and between themselves and their institutions—that will not differ much in their content from those in the holistic model. Therefore, it may happen that even though H^1 is not equivalent to $I,^1$ H^2 may be equivalent to $I,^2$ and H^3 to $I.^3$ To prove this, let us consider two scenarios. The first concerns $I,^2$ the second element in the individualistic model; the second concerns $I.^3$

In the first scenario, individuals (I^1) who have their own standards of rationality decide as free agents to shape human relations in a way that creates a superhuman agency with its distinctive standards of rationality. The superhuman agency determines the relations among them according to these standards (I^2). The result of this arrangement is similar to that offered by Rousseau in his *Social Contract*. In the community led by the general will, that is, the community which plays the role of such an agency, the legislator,

> who dares to undertake the establishment of a people should feel that he is, so to speak, in a position to change human nature, to transform each individual (who by himself is a perfect and solitary whole), into a part of a larger whole from which this individual receives, in a sense, his life and his being; to alter man's constitution in order to strengthen it; to substitute a partial and moral existence for the physical and independent existence we have all received from nature. In a word, he must deny man his own forces in order to give him forces that are alien to him and that he cannot make use of without the help of others.[21]

Comparing social relations between individuals in this individualistic model (I^2) and in the holistic one (H^2) illustrates that they do not necessarily differ in their content. Accordingly, despite the fact that they arise from opposing conceptual frameworks it is possible that I^2 is equivalent to $H,^2$ even though I^1 is not equivalent to $H.^1$ Therefore, I^2 cannot offer a definitive alternative to H^2; to that extent methodological individualism does not provide a comprehensive alternative to holism.

In the second scenario, individuals (I^1) who have their own standards of rationality decide as free agents to create relations among themselves (I^2) such that they maintain their individual standards of rationality. They also decide to establish social institutions that act according to their individual

The Controversy

standards. However, they decide to give up the possibility of reimposing their individual standards of rationality upon those institutions if the institutions cease to act according to these standards. Thus, the relations between the individuals and these institutions are permanent and resistance to the latter is precluded. This means that the individuals create a superhuman agency with its own distinctive standards of rationality. The superhuman agency determines forever the relations between them and itself according to these standards (I^3). This arrangement resembles, in its essence, that presented by Hobbes when he writes that "the subjects cannot change the forme of government," since

> they that have already Instituted a Commonwealth, being thereby bound by Convenant, to own the actions, and Judgements of one, cannot lawfully make a new Covenant, among themselves, to be obedient to any other, in any thing whatsoever, without his permission.[22]

Again, comparing I^3 with H^3 illustrates that the content of one does not necessarily differ from the other. Individuals can resolve to surrender control of their institutions, giving up the right to reform those institutions even if they deviate from their intended purpose. If they do, then their situation resembles that of individuals in the holistic model, who are unable to challenge or reform these institutions. Accordingly, despite the fact that they arise from opposite conceptual frameworks, it is possible that I^3 may be equivalent to H^3, even if I^1 is not equivalent to H^1, nor I^2 equivalent to H^2. Therefore, I^3 cannot offer a definitive alternative to H^3; again, to that extent methodological individualism does not offer a comprehensive alternative to holism.

In both of these individualistic scenarios for establishing social relations, contingent arrangements may undermine the responsiveness of the institutions thus established to the individuals who established them. This shows that in the individualistic model social relations may pass beyond the control of individuals, as is the case in the holistic model. Indeed, in both models, there is room for a superhuman agency with its own distinctive standards of rationality. It is for this reason that the contractarian rather than the individualistic explanatory model constitutes the most comprehensive alternative to the holistic one. The contractarian model does not allow the emergence of any superhuman agency with its distinctive standards of rationality. It establishes relations (both among individuals in the act of social contract proper, and between individuals and their institutions in the act of creating government, in the act of political trusteeship, or in another way) that serve useful functions while permitting individuals to preserve and maintain their own standards of rationality, and while leaving them capable, as free agents, of reimposing those standards upon the social institutions.

Given the three elements in the contractarian model—human agency or the individuals themselves and their standards of rationality (C^1), the relations among individuals (C^2), and the relations between them and the social institutions created by them (C^3)—the comparison between the individualistic and the contractarian model runs as follows: I^1 is equivalent to C^1 (since the contractarian model always has an individualistic framework) but I^2 may or may not be equivalent to C^2 and I^3 may or may not be equivalent to C^3. However, the comparison between the contractarian and holistic model is always: C^1 is not equivalent to H^1, nor is C^2 equivalent to H^2, or C^3 to H^3.

It would be a mistake to claim that if the contractarian model offers a comprehensive and successful alternative to the holistic model, then the doctrine of any thinker who enjoys the reputation of a contractarian can offer such an alternative to the doctrine of any other thinker who is considered a holist. In other words, it would be a mistake to assume that any two doctrines, one contractarian and the other holistic, will always be as comprehensively opposed as the versions of contractarianism and holism presented in Locke's *Two Treatises* and Filmer's *Patriarcha*. In order to fully appreciate the uniqueness of the conceptual dimension of the controversy between Locke and Filmer, it is necessary to draw a distinction between broadly defined holistic and contractarian *traditions*, on the one hand, and more particular, exacting holistic and contractarian *models* on the other.

By tradition I mean here a broad category of positions—a category with loosely defined characteristics. The conditions necessary for membership in a tradition need not be exact; they need only define a general similarity in certain elements which is sufficient to place a position displaying such elements into a tradition. In contrast, my use of the term model is meant to include those doctrines whose explanatory elements display a particular structure. Membership in a model type requires rigorous adherence of these elements to this structure. The requirements of membership in a model are thus stricter than those of a tradition. Not all explanatory models of the same tradition will fall into the same model type.

To clarify this, let us look more closely at the holistic and contractarian traditions, contrasting them with holistic and contractarian models. The holistic tradition is based upon an approach that looks to some sort of superhuman agency as the basic unit that underlines any explanation of social relations. To this tradition belong such thinkers as Plato, the medieval upholders of the divine right of kings, Filmer, Hegel, and Marx. The points of departure of their accounts of social relations are, respectively, the Greek polis, the will of God, paternal power, the Absolute Spirit, and productive forces. Their styles of political thinking share a deterministic vision of social life and the place of individuals in it.

The contractarian tradition is based upon an approach that looks to human agency as the basic unit that underlies any explanation of social relations. This tradition includes such thinkers as Suarez, Hobbes, Locke, Rousseau, Kant, and Rawls. The points of departure of their accounts of social relations are always individuals who are situated outside of institutional social ties—that is, individuals in the state of nature or in the original position. These thinkers share a voluntarist vision of social life and the place of individuals in it.

A thinker belongs to the holistic tradition if his doctrine embraces at least one of the elements of the holistic model: H_1, H_2 or H_3. Similarly, a thinker belongs to the contractarian tradition if his doctrine includes at least one of the elements of the contractarian model: C_1, C_2 or C_3. However, the affiliation of various thinkers to one or the other of these traditions—holistic or contractarian—need not be equally strong. The strength of a particular thinker's affiliation to a tradition depends upon the particular elements included in his doctrine. Within the holistic tradition the inclusion of element H_1 is of greater importance than the inclusion of either of the other elements alone, or even of both together, since H_1 sets the conceptual premises of the tradition. Similarly, within the contractarian tradition, the inclusion of element C_1 is of greater importance than the inclusion of either of the other elements alone, or even of both together, since C_1 lays down contractarianism's conceptual foundations. The affiliation of one thinker to the holistic tradition will be stronger than the affiliation of another to the same tradition if the doctrine of the first includes H_1 alone and that of the second includes H_2 or H_3 or H_2 and H_3—but not H_1. Similarly, the affiliation of one thinker to the contractarian tradition will be stronger than the affiliation of another to the same tradition if the doctrine of the first includes C_1 alone and that of the second includes only C_2 or C_3 or C_2 and C_3.

It may well happen that one thinker belongs to both the holistic and contractarian traditions. This is the case when his doctrine includes elements of both the holistic and contractarian models of explanation. However, one thinker cannot have an equally strong affiliation to both these traditions, since both H_1 and C_1 cannot be included in the same argument, and since the presence of one or the other in a doctrine always indicates a stronger affiliation to one or the other tradition. For example, the doctrine of Aquinas includes H^1 (since there is a superhuman agency with its own standards of rationality—God) and H^2 (since social relations in which individuals find themselves are determined by God according to his standards of rationality). At the same time, the doctrine of Aquinas embraces C^3 (since the relations between the people and their social institutions are man-made and reflect human standards of rationality and therefore may be altered by the people according to their own standards of rationality, even to the point of active opposition to tyranny). Aquinas' doctrine thus includes elements of both the holistic and contractarian models: H^1, H^2 and C^3. Accordingly, Aquinas belongs to both the holistic and contractarian traditions but since his doctrine includes H^1 his affiliation to the holistic tradition is stronger than his affiliation to the contractarian.[23] The doctrine of Rousseau, on the other hand, takes as its starting point C^1 (individuals who have their own standards of rationality). Yet its second element is H^2 (since individuals shape human relations in a way that creates a superhuman agency with its distinctive standards of rationality and the superhuman agency—the community led by the general will—determines the relations among them according to these standards). Rousseau's third element is contractarian: C^3 (since the community led by the general will establishes the government and is able to alter its relations with that government according to the standards of its own rationality—which includes the removal of the government "when it becomes incompatible with the public good"[24]). Rousseau's doctrine thus includes elements of both the holistic and contractarian models: C^1, H^2 and C^3. Accordingly, Rousseau, like Aquinas, belongs to both traditions. Yet Rousseau's affiliation to the contractarian tradition is stronger than his affiliation to the holistic one.[25]

It becomes clear, then, that the affiliation of a doctrine to one tradition does not automatically make its author an opponent of the opposite tradition. This is the case because in each of these traditions conclusions may be reached that contradict the conceptual premises underlying the tradition. Indeed, each tradition has room for doctrines that include elements of the opposing tradition—that is, in the holistic tradition we can find C^2 and C^3 coupled with H^1, and in the contractarian tradition we can find H^2 and H^3 with C^1.

Thus, the holistic and contractarian traditions cannot be said to comprehensively and successfully oppose each other; only the more precisely defined holistic and contractarian models can be said to do so. This is due to the very structure of these models. The holistic model always consists of H^1

H^2 and H^3 while the contractarian model always consists of C^1, C^2 and C^3.

Clearly, the holistic model is a subset of the holistic tradition and the contractarian model is a subset of the contractarian tradition. The holistic model always shares with the holistic tradition the basic element H^1, and the contractarian model always shares with the contractarian tradition the basic element C^1. Thus, the membership of an author in the holistic tradition is a necessary though not sufficient condition for his developing a holistic model, and the membership of an author in the contractarian tradition is a necessary though not sufficient condition for his developing a contractarian model.

One of my purposes in comparing the holistic and contractarian traditions with holistic and contractarian models is that certain thinkers have been affiliated with and perceived as representatives of each of these traditions, yet have not produced consistent models. For example, some of the most prominent pillars of the contractarian tradition—Hobbes, Rousseau, and Kant—have failed to consistently adhere to the contractarian model.

Hobbes' doctrine embraces C^1 (since there are individuals who have their own standards of rationality), C^2 (since these individuals decide to establish social relations according to their individual standards of rationality), and H^3 (they create a superhuman agency with its own distinctive standards of rationality and this agency determines the relations between them and itself according to these standards). Thus, Hobbes' doctrine deviates from the contractarian model (C^1, C^2 and C^3). Rousseau's doctrine embraces C^1 (since there are individuals who have their own standards of rationality), H^2 (since individuals shape human relations in a way that creates the community led by the general will, that is, a superhuman agency with distinctive standards of rationality, and this agency determines the relations among individuals according to these standards), and C^3 (since the community led by the general will establishes its institutions and is able to alter its relations with these institutions according to its standards of rationality). Thus, Rousseau's doctrine also deviates from the contractarian model (C^1, C^2 and C^3). Finally, Kant's doctrine embraces C^1 (since there are individuals who have their own standards of rationality), C^2 (since these individuals decide to establish social relations in accordance with their individual standards of rationality), and H^3 (since they create a superhuman agency with its own distinctive standards of rationality and this agency determines the relations between them and itself according to these standards). Kant's adoption of H^3 is clear, since in his doctrine (as in that of Hobbes) rebellion is precluded. Kant takes pains to justify this point:

The reason is that the people, under an existing civil constitution, has no longer any right to judge how the constitution would be administrated. For if we suppose that it does have this right to judge and that it disagrees with the judgement of the actual head of state, who is to decide which side is right? Neither can act as judge of his own cause. Thus there should have to be another head above the head of state to mediate between the latter and the people, which is self-contradictory.[26]

Thus, Kant's doctrine also deviates from the contractarian model (C^1, C^2 and C^3).

Hobbes, Rousseau, and Kant (among others) have failed to adhere to the contractarian model since each eventually changed the source of standards of rationality from individuals to a superhuman agency. Whatever this superhuman agency is—Hobbes' sovereign, Rousseau's community led by the general will, or Kant's civil government—its standards or will always support the standards of individuals as the supreme guide to social life. In failing to construct a consistent contractarian model, each of these thinkers adopted what Jean Hampton calls an "alienation social contract theory." The essence of this alienation is the individuals' loss of their status as agents—a status that they enjoyed before entering the social contract. After such a contract is enacted, individuals are governed by a superhuman agency of which they have become a part.[27]

The reason such thinkers as Suarez, Locke, and Rawls managed to work out consistent contractarian models embracing C^1, C^2 and C^3 should now be clear. They did not, at any stage of their arguments, propose any kind of conversion of the individuals' standards of rationality into the standards of any superhuman agency. Accordingly, the standards of rationality of the individuals entering the social contract remain, for these thinkers, the supreme guide to action in social life. Thus, the thinkers who produced consistent contractarian models adopted—to use Hampton's terminology once again—an "agency social contract theory," in which individuals maintain their status as agents after entering the contract.[28]

Drawing a distinction between traditions and models permits us to better appreciate the conceptual dimension of the controversy between Filmer and Locke, and supports the claim that this controversy holds a unique position in the history of political thought.

The traditions of holism and contractarianism have dominated the history of political thought. The clash between them is inevitable, since each is based upon conceptual premises that are irreconcilable with those that underlie the other. However, in the works of some of the most prominent representatives of these traditions (especially those on the contractarian side) the sharpness of this clash has been obscured by the basic incompatibility between the primary elements or starting points of their doctrines and their subsequent elements—by the inclusion of holistic and contractarian elements together in the same doctrine. Although other distinguished thinkers managed to avoid such inconsistencies by developing consistent holistic and contractarian models in their respective traditions, they were not usually concerned with contrasting holism and contractarianism. Rather, they used holistic and contractarian models as tools in pursuing their own projects—for example, that of explaining the process of universal history (in Hegel's case) or giving an account of the concept of justice (in Rawls' case). Accordingly, holists and contractarians who did develop consistent models usually did not make use of them in direct polemics against their opponents. Thus, they did not confront the direct challenge of their strongest opposition.

The importance of the controversy between Filmer and Locke lies in the fact that it offered a clash between the holistic and contractarian traditions and models (that is, between H^1, H^2, H^3 and C^1, C^2, C^3) in the sharpest form of polemic: the refutation of his adversary's model was the top priority of each thinker. Accordingly, unlike holists and contractarians that preceded and followed them, neither Filmer nor Locke created his doctrine within the comfortable isolation of his own tradition; instead, each shaped his system under the direct pressure and challenge of opposition (in Filmer's case, from his contractarian contemporaries, such as Philip Hunton;[29] in Locke's case, from Filmer). This setting led both thinkers, on the one hand, to a remarkable concentration on the opposition's explanatory model and the argument in support of it, and, on the other, to the maximal refinement of his own as well as concern for his model's consistency. It is due to these two factors that the controversy between Locke and Filmer offers a unique view that exposes the depth of the disagreement between holism and contractarianism.

Summary

My intent in this chapter was to set down the framework of the controversy between Filmer and Locke, which will be explored in detail in the chapters that follow.

Discussing the conceptual dimension of the controversy has made it possible for me to present Filmer's and Locke's systems as (respectively) essentially holistic and contractarian. I have done this by establishing, first, that the essence of Filmerism is not patriarchalism but holism and, second, that it is not methodological individualism but contractarianism that constitutes the appropriate counterpart of holism. In light of these two conclusions, we can see that Filmer's and Locke's systems are much more sophisticated than is generally admitted in scholarship. Indeed, presenting Filmer's system as essentially holistic and not patriarchalistic shows that its conceptual framework and the complexity of its argumentation surpasses mainstream patriarchalist thought much more than, for example, Schochet assumes.[30] Similarly, the realization that Locke's system includes a contractarian model of explanation in order to comprehensively and successfully oppose Filmer's holistic model shows that its conceptual framework and the complexity of its argumentation surpasses those of other contemporary contractarians (more so, for instance, then Martyn P. Thompson assumes[31]). Moreover, by presenting contractarianism as the appropriate counterpart to holism I have been able to reinterpret the conceptual background and significance of the controversy between Filmer and Locke in the history of political thought. Instead of discussing the holistic and contractarian traditions and arguments separately (as do Sir Karl Popper, Otto Gierke, and Gierke's British followers Sir Ernest Barker and J. W. Gough[32]), I have presented these traditions and models jointly and in relation to each other in order to indicate the depth of their disagreement and to distill from each the definitive arguments of holism and contractarianism.

---

[1] See Peter Laslett, "Introduction" in Robert Filmer, *Patriarcha and Other Political Works of Sir Robert Filmer,* Peter Laslett, ed. (Oxford: Basil Blackwell, 1949) and Peter Laslett, "Introduction" in John Locke, *Two Treatises of Government,* Peter Laslett, ed. (Cambridge: Cambridge University Press, 1960). In this book, I refer to Laslett's 1988 edition of the Two Treatises

[2] Gordon G. Schochet, *Patriarchalism in Political Thought* (Oxford: Basil Blackwell, 1975), p. 1.

[3] Ibid.

[4] Peter Laslett, *The World We Have Lost: English Society Before the Coming of Industry* (London: Methuen, 1965).

[5] J.C.D. Clark, *English Society 1688-1832: Ideology, Social Structure and Political Practice during the Ancient Regime* (Cambridge: Cambridge University Press, 1985).

[6] Schochet, *Patriarchalism in Political Thought,* pp. 81-82.

[7] R.W.K. Hinton, "Husbands, Fathers and Conquerors," in *Political Studies,* XV, (1967): 291-300.

The Controversy 21

⁸James Daly, *Sir Robert Filmer and English Political Thought* (Toronto: Toronto University Press, 1979), p. 13.
⁹Ibid. p. 152.
¹⁰Ibid. p. 153.
¹¹See Laslett, "Introduction" in Locke, *Two Treatises of Government*, pp. 67-79.
¹²See sec. III of this chapter, where I argue that Hobbes and Locke belong to the same contractarian tradition, as opposed to the holistic tradition, which Filmer represents.
¹³W.H. Greenleaf, *Order, Empiricism and Politics: Two Traditions of English Political Thought 1500-1700* (Westport, Connecticut: Greenwood Press, 1980), p. 87.
¹⁴The main body of Filmer's system emerged from his support for the royalist cause at the time of the English Civil War. Its beginnings can be traced back to the years 1635-1642, when his most famous work, *Patriarcha: A Defence of the Natural Power of Kings against the Unnatural Liberty of the People*, is believed to have been produced. Patriarcha was not published during the lifetime of its author, but a handwritten copy was circulated among the manors of the gentry of Kent. It was followed by other conceptually related works. In 1648, Filmer attacked in print William Prynne's *Sovereign Power of Parliaments and Kingdoms* and published *The Freeholder's Grand Inquest Touching Our Sovereigne Lord the King and His Parliament*. The book became an influential source of royalist argument and was immediately followed by *The Anarchy of a Limited Monarchy*, which embodied a rejection of Philip Hunton's *Treatise of Monarchie* and his *Vindication*. Also in 1648, Filmer published a collection of carefully chosen extracts from Jean Bodin called *The Necessity of the Absolute Power of All Kings: And in particular of the King of England*. After 1649, when royalist writing virtually disappeared from the spectrum of English political thought, Filmer stood alone against Milton, Hobbes, and even Grotius in defending the lost cause of the executed monarch in his *Observations concerning the Original of Government, upon Mr. Hobs Leviathan, Mr. Milton against Salmasius, H. Grotius De Jure Belli* (1652). Accompanying the collection was Filmer's *Observations Upon Aristotle's Politics Touching Forms of Government*, a strong pro-absolutist attack upon Aristotle and, indeed, upon the main body of the Aristotelian tradition in political thought. The last political work he wrote was a short paper, *Directions for Obedience to Government in dangerous or doubtful Times* (1653), in which he analyzed the extent to which the subjects of a lawful king were obliged to a usurper. In the last decade of Stuart rule (1679-1688), Filmer's works appeared in numerous editions and his system became the official ideology of the monarchy, and was thus supported by the authority of state and Church.
¹⁵Locke formulated the principles of his system while involved in the so-called Exclusion controversy (1679-1683). While trying to impose the succession to the throne of the unpopular, Catholic, pro-French James, Duke of York, the Court met with the opposition of the well-organized, popular Whig movement led by Earl

Shaftesbury. Supporting the Whig cause, Locke, a close associate and intellectual companion of Shaftesbury, aimed his *Two Treatises* against the main body of Filmerism, which was chosen by the Court to justify its absolutist position. (For the efforts to determine the precise time of Locke's composition of the *Two Treatises,* see Laslett's Introduction to the *Two Treatises,* pp. 45-66 and Richard Ashcraft, *Revolutionary Politics and Locke's Two Treatises of Government* [Princeton: Princeton University Press, 1986]).

[16] In drawing this distinction I follow Susan James, *The Content of Social Explanation* (Cambridge: Cambridge University Press, 1984), chs. II and III.

[17] "Holism means that some superhuman agents or factors are supposed to be at work in history," J.W.N. Watkins, "Historical Explanation in the Social Sciences" in J. O'Neill, ed. *Modes of Individualism and Collectivism* (London: Heinemann Educational, 1973), p. 168.

[18] It is impossible to escape the use of societal concepts in attempting to understand some aspects of individual behaviour: concepts involving the notions of status and role cannot themselves be reduced to a conjunction of statements in which these or other societal concepts do not appear." M. Mandelbaum, "Societal Facts," in J. O'Neill, ed. *Modes of Individualism and Collectivism* (London: Heinemann Educational, 1973), p. 225. Compare also D.H. Ruben, "The Existence of Social Entities," in *Philosophical Quarterly* 32 (1982): 295-310. For a classic statement of this notion, see F.H. Bradley, "My Station and its Duties," in F.H. Bradley, *Ethical Studies* (London: H.S. King, 1876), p. 158.

[19] "There is no other way toward an understanding of social phenomena but through our understanding of individual actions directed toward other people and guided by their expected behaviour," F.A. Hayek, *Individualism and Economic Order* (London: Routledge and K. Paul, 1949), p. 6. "All social phenomena, and especially the functioning of all social institutions, should always be understood as resulting from the decisions, actions, attitudes, etc., of human individuals," Karl Popper, *The Open Society and Its Enemies* (London: G. Routledge and Sons Ltd, 1945), vol. II, p. 98; "Methodological individualism means that human beings are supposed to be the only moving agents in history," Watkins, "Historical Explanation in the Social Sciences," p. 168.

[20] "A theoretical understanding of an abstract social structure should be derived from the more empirical beliefs about concrete individuals" J.W.N. Watkins, "Ideal Types and Historical Explanation," in J. O'Neill, ed. *Modes of Individualism and Collectivism* (London: Heinemann Educational, 1973), p. 151. Compare D.H. Mellor, "The Reduction of Society," *Philosophy* 57 (1982): 51-75.

[21] Jean Jacques Rousseau, *On the Social Contract; Discourse on the Origin of Inequality; Discourse on Political Economy,* translated and edited by Donald A. Cress, introduced by Peter Gay (Indianapolis, Indiana: Hackett Publishing Company, 1983), bk. II, ch. VII.

[22] Thomas Hobbes, *Leviathan,* C.B. Macpherson, ed. (Harmondsworth: Penguin, 1985), ch. XVIII.

[23] For a discussion of Aquinas as a distinguished representative of contractarianism, see Ernest Barker, "Introduction" in Ernest Barker, ed. *Social Contract* (Oxford: Oxford University Press, 1971), pp. VIII-IX.

[24] Rousseau, *The Social Contract,* bk. III, ch. XVIII.

[25] For a discussion of Rousseau within the holistic tradition, see Lucio Colletti, *From Rousseau to Lenin: Studies in Ideology and Society* (New York and London: Monthly Review Press, 1972).

[26] Immanuel Kant, "On the Common Saying: 'This May Be True in Theory, But It Does Not Apply in Practice.'" in Hans Reiss, ed., *Kant's Political Writings* (Cambridge: Cambridge University Press, 1970), p. 81.

[27] Jean Hampton, *Hobbes and the Social Contract Tradition* (Cambridge: Cambridge University Press, 1986), ch. IX.

[28] Hampton sees Locke as a typical representative of agency social contract theory. See ibid., pp. 267-79.

[29] Most of Filmer's criticism of the contractarian argument takes place in his attack on Hunton's work. See footnote 14 above.

[30] Schochet discusses Filmer's system together with those of his contemporary patriarchalists, such as, for example, John Spelman, Dully Digges, and John Maxwell. See Schochet, *Patriarchalism in Political Thought,* ch. VI.

[31] Thompson discusses Locke's system together with those of William Atwood, Robert Ferguson, Algernon Sidney, and James Tyrrell. See Martyn P. Thompson, *Ideas of Contract in English Political Thought in the Age of John Locke* (New York & London: Garland Publishing, 1987).

[32] See Popper, *The Open Society and Its Enemies;* Otto Gierke, *Natural Law and the Theory of Society, 1500-1800* (Cambridge: Cambridge University Press, 1934); Ernest Barker, "Introduction" in Ernest Barker, ed. Social Contract; J.W. Gough, *The Social Contract* (Oxford: Clarendon Press,1957).

Chapter 2

The State of Nature

We can now move on to a more detailed presentation of the ways in which Filmer and Locke prepared the foundations of their holistic and contractarian models. Filmer positioned the basic element of his system, paternal power or superhuman agency (H^1), in the context of the biblical creation legend. Locke also provided a theological setting for his system; he based his fundamental element, individual or human agency (C^1), on the relation between God and man.[1] Both thinkers then proceed to present the standards of rationality of these agencies. Filmer demonstrated the distinctive standards of rationality of his paternal power by pointing to its operation in the social context, of which it was the backbone. Locke showed the particular standards of rationality of individuals by referring to their conduct in the social context in which they naturally found themselves.

To elaborate on this issue, in this chapter I shall analyze the relations between right and wrong, right and might, and norms and facts in Filmer's holism and Locke's contractarianism. I shall argue that despite the Christian setting of Filmer's system, in principle, the presence and operation of paternal power rules out the possibility of distinguishing these three categories. Locke, for his part, puts forward the notion of the state of nature in order to reject Filmer's position, to separate right from wrong, right from might, and norms from facts, and to conceptualize the various relations among them in the situations in which human agents operate.

Filmer situates the foundation of his system, the superhuman agency or paternal power, in a theological framework. Taking the Bible, and especially the events recorded in Genesis, as the key source of historico-philosophical knowledge, he refers to the creation legend and claims that God established paternal power in paradise.[2] It was this power that shaped the relations among the members of the first human family. Accordingly, Adam, in whom God vested paternal power, was father and ruler, Eve was his wife and subject, and their offspring were his children and subjects. Filmer maintains that paternal power is an object transferred to Adam's heirs—that is, to all contemporary rulers. Indeed, "all power on earth is either derived or usurped from the fatherly power, there being no other original to be found of any power whatsoever."[3] Thus, Filmer concludes, contemporary rulers exercise the same power Adam exercised over his family and that same power shapes all contemporary human relations. The ties between a ruler and his subjects are like those between a father and other members of his family. In other words, there is no society: there is only the patriarchal family. Moreover, there is no state, only the ruler's household. Like Adam, contemporary rulers are absolute monarchs, and the only legitimate form of government is absolute monarchy.[4]

Having introduced paternal power as the backbone of his holistic system, Filmer moves on to establish its standards of rationality, expressing the relations between right and wrong, and right and might. He assumes that there is an objective difference between these categories (as he was obliged to do as a Christian writer), but he fails to apply this distinction in his system. To justify his apparent failing, Filmer insists that a distinction be drawn between the two systems of law according to which monarchs and their subjects are judged—the law of nature and the positive law. He admits that the law of nature provides an objective criterion of right and wrong and, in his polemic against Grotius, maintains that it deserves this status in view of its origin in the will of God and its binding force upon all rulers and ruled alike. Indeed, though "the term jus naturae is not originally to be found in scripture," Filmer agrees that "the law of nature or the divine law in general... comprehends some principles of morality notoriously known of themselves." Accordingly, he states that,

> the same commandment that forbids one private man to rob another, or one corporation to hurt another corporation, obliges also one King not to rob another King, and one commonwealth not to spoil another: the same law that enjoins charity to all men, even to enemies, binds princes and states to show charity to one another, as well as private persons.[5]

Although Filmer does not further elaborate on the law of nature, this passage alone establishes two basic points concerning its content. First, the Filmerian concept of the law of nature contains an objective distinction between right and wrong. For example, an individual is morally right when he offers charity to others; he is morally wrong when he robs or hurts others. Second, the Filmerian concept of the law of nature contains an objective distinction between right and might. For example, an individual has a right (or claim) to charity on the part of others, yet he has no right (or claim) to the property or bodies of others. That is, when an individual robs or hurts another, he does so not because he has a right or a claim to the other's property or body, but because he has sufficient might to rob or hurt him.

Nevertheless, putting aside Filmer's obviously modified position in his later political works,[6] the natural distinction between right and wrong and right and might plays no role whatsoever in his consideration of the everyday life of monarchs and their subjects. According to Filmer, the fact that God granted paternal power to Adam and thenceforth to all other rulers entails that the ruled are cut off from the direct binding force of the law of nature.[7] The only natural institution and natural authority that they are obliged to obey is paternal power itself. In turn, the natural prerogative of the holders of paternal power is to act and to pass positive law only according their own wills.[8] Therefore, as Filmer stresses, no subject can judge "what law is contrary to God's will, or to nature, or to reason,"[9] since "what laws are upright and what evil" is to be judged exclusively by the king.[10] In other words, the ruled are always subordinate to the will of the rulers. To justify this, Filmer argues that in terrestrial life monarchs are right to judge their subjects according to the provisions of positive law, since in the next life, when the monarchs themselves are judged by God according to the law of nature, they also will be held personally responsible for the deeds of the subjects who followed their commands.[11]

The impossibility of judging whether the ruler's will is right or wrong in Filmer's system implies that it is also impossible to distinguish between right and might in Filmer's account of political practice. There are two senses in which right and might are inseparable under Filmer's system. First, they are technically inseparable: that is, they cannot be found in separate persons or institutions. Right and might are vested exclusively in paternal power, and are thus always on the side of its holders. That is to say, there is no external barrier—either normative or empirical—to utilization of this power by the rulers. Indeed, in Filmer, there is no other right or might to oppose the possessors of paternal power. Filmer makes this point very clear in his attack upon Hobbes' *Leviathan*, stressing the incompatibility of "the right of nature [that is]... a liberty for each man to use his own power as he will himself for preservation of his own life" with the dominion that God gave to Adam.[12] Further, right and might are conceptually inseparable: a distinction between them within paternal power itself is impossible. This dimension of the inseparability of right and might removes any internal barrier to exercising paternal power; it implies that when one has might at one's disposal one automatically also has a right. Filmer stresses this issue in his polemic against Hobbes, pointing out the inconsistencies of his account. Filmer asks: "how can [a conqueror] get a right of sovereignty by conquest when... he himself hath [no] right to conquer?"[13] If he managed to conquer, Filmer argues, it was because he had might at his disposal which automatically means he had the right as well.

To sum up Filmer's position, when the nominal, natural law separation between right and wrong and right and might is applied to actual political practice, it is impossible to distinguish between the normative and descriptive parts of his doctrine. Since subjects are not required to act upon natural law in political practice, and since they are always required to obey paternal power, then from Filmer's perspective there is no distinction between what a monarch should do and what he does, and no distinction between what his subjects should do and what they do when they follow his will. In other words, according to Filmer, facts and norms do not differ in their terrestrial status. The role of human beings—of subjects, at least—is to accept the way things are as the way they ought to be.

Rejecting the position of his adversary, Locke begins by situating the foundation of his system, human agency or the individual, in direct relation to God. Man is, Locke claims, the workmanship of God.[14] God not only created him, not only sent him into the world, but also provided him with standards of rationality, which express the relations between right and wrong, and right and might. Locke insists that these standards are to be found in the law of nature, which is the will of God, and which is knowable by reason or revelation.[15]

Locke bases the content of the law of nature on the workmanship model.[16] The act of creation gives God a natural right over man, who is God's property.[17] God's natural right creates natural duty on the part of man: the duty to preserve himself and the rest of mankind,[18] which includes a duty to preserve society.[19] Locke makes this point clear when he endorses the biblical Golden Rule as the "chief law of nature and bond of every society":[20] "Our Saviour's great rule, that 'we should love our neighbour as ourselves' is such a fundamental truth for the regulating of human society, that, I think, by that alone, one might without difficulty determine

The State of Nature

all the cases and doubts in social morality."[21]

The body of the law of nature provides Locke with an objective distinction between right and wrong, and right and might. Indeed, the imperative of self-preservation, which is the pillar of this law, does not express man's subjective desire to preserve his being, but is the expression of God's objective will[22] to preserve mankind as a whole; it does not arise in an ethical vacuum, as in Hobbes,[23] but is a component of a coherent moral system.[24] Thus, for example, when man preserves his life or that of his fellow men he is morally right; when he takes his life or theirs he is morally wrong. Similarly, he has a right (or claim) to expect from others the preservation of his life and that of his fellow men, yet he has no right (or claim) to take his life or theirs. That is, when he takes his life or theirs, he does so not because he has a right or a claim to these lives, but because he has sufficient might to take them.

Having established an objective distinction between right and wrong and right and might, Locke moves on to argue that, contrary to Filmer's account, this distinction is not nominal but real and, as such, can be applied in social and political practice. Following seventeenth century natural law theorists, he introduces the classical notion of the state of nature, which alone—regardless of its particular form—challenges Filmer's position on two fundamental issues. First, in the state of nature the law of nature is binding directly. Second, in this state there is no power recognized by and exercised over all individuals, groups, institutions, or states. However, in presenting his own version of the state of nature, Locke goes beyond these issues to discuss the various relations between right and wrong, right and might, as well as norms and facts.

Locke assumes that the right of self-preservation that belongs to every man under the law of nature must be accompanied by the necessary might to guarantee its implementation. Indeed, "the *Law of Nature* would, as all other Laws that concern Men in this World, be in vain, if there were no body that in the State of Nature, had a *Power to Execute* that Law."[25] Accordingly, the Lockean man has two natural powers at his disposal. The first is the power to arrange "*whatsoever he thought fit for the Preservation of himself*, and the rest of Mankind," within the permission of the law of nature; therefore, everyone is entitled to defend his life, liberty, and estate against others. The second is the power to judge and punish those who break this law.[26]

At this point, Locke clarifies the relations between right, might, and power. In his system, a right enjoys a normative status and as such is unequivocally a moral category. The status of the concept of might is less straightforward: it is primarily understood as a physical capacity to use force; nevertheless, it is not a morally indifferent concept. If might supports a right, then it takes on the normative status and moral character of that right; if it is aimed against a right, then it lacks the status and character of that right. In the latter case, Locke describes might in terms of force and violence; he does not call it power. In Locke, although he is not always consistent, the term "power" has a special meaning quite different from contemporary ordinary usage: power is that might which preserves right. Throughout the *Two Treatises,* the term is generally reserved for this purpose. Paternal power is for Locke a "Privilege of Children,"[27] who are governed for their own good.[28] Despotical power stems from "the *Right of War*—a liberty to kill the aggressor"[29]—and therefore from "the Right to destroy" that which threatens the innocent person with destruction.[30] Political power is grounded in the two natural powers of individuals: to preserve themselves and to punish those who violate natural law; these two powers, in turn, are derived from the individual natural right of self-preservation.[31]

It is important to remember that might which is not based upon a right is not legitimate, no matter how effective it may be. That is to say, might by itself is not legitimate, and therefore is not power. Moreover, any power enjoys its normative status and moral character whether or not it is sufficient for the defense of the right that it serves. The best example of this is to be found in Locke's discussion of the case of the Greek Christians. He writes that all people "who were forced to submit to the Yoke of a Government by constraint, have always a Right to shake it off, and free themselves from the Usurpation, or Tyranny, which the Sword hath brought in upon them, till their Rulers put them under such a Frame of Government, as they willingly, and of choice consent to," and, turning to the case of Greeks, adds, "who doubts but the Grecian Christians, descendants of the ancient possessors of that Country may justly cast off the Turkish yoke."[32]

There are three possible relations between right and might: might may perfectly preserve right; might may preserve right imperfectly, or at least not oppose it; or might may threaten right. The law of nature is upheld in the first two situations. In fact, Locke distinguishes two varieties of the state of nature (following Pufendorf) based on these two situations: the first situation is the state of nature proper; the second is the ordinary state of nature.[33] The third situation, in which the law of nature is replaced by "another Rule," that of "Force and Violence," is the state of war.

The only might to be found in Locke's state of nature proper is that of the two natural powers: the law of nature is here so perfectly executed that facts always conform entirely to it. The state of nature proper is therefore the condition in which reality fully conforms to the moral principles of this law; there is no difference between how people should act and how they do act. Using this explanatory device, Locke describes the outcome of the perfect operation of his theory's fundamental moral principles; thus, the state of nature proper belongs to the normative part of his doctrine. As such, this state constitutes an *a priori* hypothesis that escapes any attempt at empirical verification.[34]

The state of nature proper is, in fact, a hypothetical state in which relations among human beings are determined by notions of natural freedom and natural equality which mutually interact in the absence of any natural "Subordination or Subjection" among men.[35]

Locke describes perfect human freedom as the position of men who are able "to order their Actions, and dispose of their Possessions, and Persons as they think fit, within the bounds of the Law of Nature, without asking leave, or depending upon the Will of any other Man."[36] This concept of natural liberty can work only in conjunction with the assumption of natural equality,[37] which Locke characterizes as an "*equal Right* that every Man hath *to his Natural Freedom.*"[38] Therefore, the state of nature proper is also a condition "wherein all the Power and Jurisdiction is reciprocal, no one having more than another: there being nothing more evident, than that Creatures of the same species and rank promiscuously born to all the same advantages of Nature, and the use of the same faculties, should also be equal one amongst another."[39] Thus, on the fundamental question of rights, people are equal to one another and free from "any Superior Power on Earth, and not... under the Will or Legislative Authority of Man."[40]

Although people are born with the natural status of freedom and equality, the only guarantee of their attainment and preservation in everyday life is the rigorous following of reason, which discovers and clarifies the principles of natural law.[41] (Thus, all natural differences between people are determined by the different degrees to which natural law is known by each.) In other words, it is reason that distinguishes men from one another with respect to their natural liberty and equality.[42]

Indeed, Locke makes it very clear that freedom goes hand in hand with reason. As he puts it, "without Liberty the Understanding would be to no purpose: And without Understanding, Liberty... would signify nothing."[43] Real freedom can only be achieved within the bounds of natural law because "*where there is no law, there is no freedom.*"[44] The opposite of the state of perfect freedom is the state of slavery, which is essentially equivalent to the state of war.[45] Men who enter into this state by aggressing against innocent men, "are not under the ties of the Common Law of Reason";[46] they lose their natural distinction of being "capable of laws" and, accordingly, their natural status as human beings. Thus it is legitimate to destroy such aggressors. Slavery "*is* nothing else, but the *State of War continued, between a lawful Conquerour, and a Captive.*"[47] The latter has no rights, and he may be killed by his master who "does him no injury by it."[48] This is an extreme argument based on Locke's concept of the relation between man and God. A captive taken in a just war (a defensive war against unlawful aggression) must have broken his relation with God (by initiating the aggression in the first place) and in this way ceased to be human. A comparison with the case of suicide is illuminating here. An individual is not allowed to commit suicide because he knows that he is "[God's] property, made to last during [God's pleasure], not [the pleasure of his fellows]."[49] In other words, a human being is obliged to maintain his relation with God by fulfilling the duty of self-preservation that forbids him to commit suicide. But as a captive taken in a just war, he lacks his previous human status since his previous relation to God has been disrupted; thus, he is no longer bound by the duty of self-preservation. As a result, he may, "by resisting the Will of his Master... draw on himself the Death he desires."[50]

The principle of natural equality is also based upon the presumption that possession of reason is required for understanding and following the directives of natural law. This principle does not seem to be affected by other "sorts of Equality," stated secondly, which are based upon age, virtue, birth, or merit,[51] since these differences exist independently of differences in rationality. Locke stresses the effects of differences in rationality; he writes that children are born to the "the full state of *Equality*"[52] but are not "Absolute Lords of their Persons and Possessions and equal to the Greatest,"[53] because all of them "are weak and helpless, without Knowledge and Understanding."[54] Natural equality therefore coexists with subjection to parents until age brings children sufficient powers of reasoning to conduct their own lives.[55] Only in this way may they attain a place equal to others within the human community. Reason is "the common bond whereby humane kind is united into one fellowship and societie."[56]

Locke's concept of natural equality implies the possibility of self-improvement and the necessity of relying on one's own faculty of reason. Apart from "*Lunaticks and Ideots*," who "are never set free from the Government of their Parents,"[57] all Lockean men, notwithstanding differences in rationality, are capable of this improvement. Man is unquestionably a social being, who owes much of his physical and intellectual growth to others, but he must answer only to God for his moral condition. In order to act according to his calling, man should cease to "neglect his understanding," and attain intellectual self-reliance.[58] The key to self-improvement,[59] is to take a critical attitude toward all human authorities, rather than "yielding to the morality of others." Neither priests, who do not permit the use of reason in explaining the principles of religion to the people,[60] nor professors, who sell "hard Words and Ignorance at a very dear rate,"[61] nor doctrinaires, who "amuze Peoples Understandings,"[62] nor even prophets, who are susceptible to "all the Extravagancies of Delusion and Error,"[63] can replace individuals in their efforts to achieve this end. "Knowing is seeing," writes Locke, "and if it be so, it is madness to persuade ourselves that we do so by another man's eyes."[64] This reliance on the sight of others is the position of those who "want no other rule of life and conduct, being satisfied with the second-hand rule which other people's conduct, opinions and advice, without any serious thinking or application, easily supply to the unwary."[65] Thus, "they who are blind will always be led by those that see, or else fall into the Ditch; and he is certainly the most subjected, the most enslaved, who is so in his Understanding."[66]

To sum up, in Locke's state of nature proper, men are naturally free and naturally equal since they use reason as best as they possibly can. Obedience to the law of nature is the only motivation for human conduct and thus right is always perfectly followed and protected by might. This feature gives the state of nature proper its normative status and moral character "as a State of Peace, Good Will, Mutual Assistance, and Preservation."[67] Only this state fully expresses the Lockean "Community of Nature,"[68] in which "the general Good" is achieved and in which everybody finds "his proper Interest."[69]

In the ordinary state of nature, on the other hand, although might does not oppose right, the execution of the law of nature, given human partiality, is not satisfactory. Accordingly, facts are far from conforming entirely to this law. Indeed, in the ordinary state of nature, reality cannot fully conform to moral principles, since "the greater part [of people are] not strict Observers of Equity and Justice."[70] The ordinary state of nature is in fact a wide spectrum of states, a number of different pictures of human behavior falling between two extremes: the state of nature proper and the state of war. What these pictures have in common is a feature that Locke describes outside the *Two Treatises* as "a state of mediocrity" where "we are not capable of living together *exactly* by a rule, nor altogether without it."[71] As such, the ordinary state of nature (unlike the state of nature proper) belongs to the descriptive part of Locke's doctrine and can be empirically verified.

Thus, the ordinary state of nature is the actual, permanent experience of human life. It includes all the relations among men that are outside the reach of civil society's political power. Locke makes this clear when he stresses that men are in the ordinary state of nature whenever they lack a common judge who could resolve controversies between them.[72] The ordinary state of nature ceases to exist only when there is a judge with the necessary authority to execute law, and when such a judge is "*indifferent* and upright" in this execution.[73] One can thus be in the ordinary state of nature with respect to certain matters, but not others, as, for example, when judges exist to resolve certain kinds of disputes, but not others. The ordinary state of nature, then, is not confined to any historical period, because "the World never was, nor ever will be, without Numbers of Men in that State,"[74] at least with regard to certain matters.

This broad conception of the ordinary state of nature allows Locke to present a long list of situations that exemplify such a state. He echoes the common view of natural law social contract theorists, writing that "all Princes and Rulers of Independent Governments" are in the state of nature with respect to one another.[75] He also suggests that the subjects of each of those princes are themselves in this state with respect to the subjects of all other princes.[76] This is also the case with two men who meet on independent territory as members of different civil societies—such as a "*Swiss* and an *Indian* in the Woods of *America*" or on a "Desert Island."[77] Moreover, since Locke assumes that the authority of civil society does not and cannot always resolve every kind of dispute that may arise among its members, he leaves room for the direct rule of natural law in civil society. This means that the state of nature is not and cannot be completely eradicated even within civil society. Indeed, to the extent that members of the same civil society do not involve the civil authority in their controversies—for example, in property disputes within the family or among neighbors—they are still in the state of nature.[78] Finally, "every *Absolute Prince*, [is in the state of nature] in respect of those who are under his *Dominion*" because, however associated, these subjects have no authority to whom they may appeal for the resolution of any dispute between them and their ruler.[79]

Winding up Locke's discussion of the concept of the state of nature and his firm distinction between its two varieties, it is important to point out their influence upon the character of his discourse, which is based upon a rigorous separation and constant interaction of right and wrong, right and might, and norms and facts. I have said that in the state of nature proper, facts conform to norms completely, while in the ordinary state of nature they do so only partially. Since the state of nature proper exists only in theory, Locke is committed to the idea that reality does not conform entirely to moral principles; yet he does not concede that this weakens the normative force of the natural law. Locke's approach is to draw a rigorous distinction between the normative and descriptive part of his doctrine and to expound his normative, contractarian argument with reference to empirically and historically verified facts. In light of this approach, the *Two Treatises* constitutes neither a compromise with political reality nor an utopian proposition.

Summary

My purpose in this chapter was to outline the relations between right and wrong, right and might, and norms and facts in Filmer and Locke. In analyzing these relations, I indicated that the fundamental opposition between their systems lies in the fact that Filmer's model implies the basic unity of these categories while Locke's includes a rigorous separation between them.

Although the state of nature is very often presented—most notably by John Dunn[80]—as an integral part of Locke's polemic with Filmer, scholarship has generally neglected the essence of this concept; it is this essence, with its clear distinction between its normative and empirical varieties, that made the polemic efficient and comprehensive. Indeed, most commentators reduce the importance of this concept either to its empirical aspects, as do, for example, Leo Strauss, Richard H. Cox, and Robert A. Goldwin,[81] or to its normative dimension, as do, for instance, Seliger and Dunn.[82] Even Richard Ashcraft, who managed to overcome this dichotomy by acknowledging both the normative and empirical elements of the state of nature, fails to see the distinction between its proper and ordinary varieties, taking the former for Locke's analysis of the law of nature and not the state of nature.[83]

---

[1]The most persuasive argument for Locke's theological world view as the set of premises for his political thought has been stated by John Dunn in his *Political Thought of John Locke* (Cambridge: Cambridge University Press, 1969) and repeated by James Tully, *A Discourse on Property: John Locke and*

his Adversaries (Cambridge: Cambridge University Press, 1980). This position now seems unchallengeable and is commonly accepted in scholarship. See, for example, Richard Ashcraft, *Locke's Two Treatises of Government* (London: Allen & Unwin, 1987), ch. 2.

[2]Compare Gordon G. Schochet, *Patriarchalism in Political Thought* (Oxford: Basil Blackwell, 1975), pp. 47-48.

[3]Robert Filmer, "Directions for Obedience to Government in Dangerous or Doubtful Times," in Robert Filmer, *Patriarcha and Other Political Works of Sir Robert Filmer,* Peter Laslett, ed. (Oxford: Basil Blackwell, 1949), p. 233.

[4]It is worth stressing the character of the relation between this theological framework and the holistic system in Filmer's doctrine. Filmer, as a Christian thinker, constructed his system in general agreement with the canons of Christianity. Indeed, in his doctrine it is God that is the creator of paternal power—Filmer's superhuman agency. As the creation of God, this superhuman agency does not challenge his omnipotence either in the terrestrial or universal dimension. Thus, Filmer's choice of holism does not make his system in any way secular. Still, God does not directly shape human relations; rather, he leaves this task to the operation of paternal power. Therefore, in this theologically situated system, the omnipotence of God does not undermine the position of the superhuman agency in creating social and political institutions.

[5]Robert Filmer, "Observations upon H. Grotius De Jure Belli et Pacis," in Robert Filmer, *Patriarcha and Other Political Works of Sir Robert Filmer,* Peter Laslett, ed. (Oxford: Basil Blackwell, 1949), p. 263.

[6]See ch. 6.

[7]See, for example, Robert Filmer, "Patriarcha," in Robert Filmer, *Patriarcha and Other Political Works of Sir Robert Filmer,* Peter Laslett, ed. (Oxford: Basil Blackwell, 1949), p. 105.

[8]Ibid., p. 96.

[9]Robert Filmer, "Observations upon Mr. Milton Against Salamasius," in Robert Filmer, *Patriarcha and Other Political Works of Sir Robert Filmer,* Peter Laslett, ed. (Oxford: Basil Blackwell, 1949), p. 257.

[10]Filmer, "Patriarcha," p. 104.

[11]Ibid., p. 105.

[12]Robert Filmer, "Observations on Mr. Hobbes' Leviathan," in Robert Filmer, *Patriarcha and Other Political Works of Sir Robert Filmer,* Peter Laslett, ed. (Oxford: Basil Blackwell, 1949), p. 241.

[13]Ibid., p. 240.

[14]It is worth outlining the character of the relation between this theological framework and the contractarian system in Locke's doctrine. Locke built his system in general agreement with Christian canons and popular beliefs. Indeed, in his doctrine it is God that is the creator of human agency. As the creation and property of God, this human agency does not challenge the omnipotence of God either in the terrestrial or universal dimension. Thus, Locke's choice of con-

tractarianism does not make his system secular. Still, in his system God does not directly shape human relationships; rather, he leaves this task to the operation of human agents. Therefore, in this theologically situated system the omnipotence of God does not undermine the position of human agency in creating social and political institutions.

[15] In principle, Locke insists that natural law is plain to rational creatures (John Locke, *Two Treatises of Government,* Peter Laslett, ed. [Cambridge: Cambridge University Press, 1960], Second Treatise, §§6, 11, 12, and 24). However, he admits that though "our mental faculties can lead us to the knowledge of this law, nevertheless it does not follow from this that all men necessarily make proper use of these faculties," (John Locke, *Essays on the Law of Nature,* Wolfgang von Leyden, ed. [Oxford: Clarendon Press, 1954], p. 133). Thus, he goes further and claims that "the greatest part cannot know [the law of nature] and therefore they must believe." (John Locke, *The Reasonableness of Christianity as delivered in the Scripture,* I.T. Ramsey, ed. [Stanford: Stanford University Press, 1958], p. 66).

[16] Locke, *Essays on the Law of Nature,* pp. 185. See also John Locke, *An Essay concerning Human Understanding,* Peter H. Niddhitch, ed. (Oxford: Clarendon Press, 1975), 2. 28. 3.

[17] Locke, *Two Treatises of Government,* Second Treatise, §6.

[18] Ibid., §§6, 7, 11, 16, 23, 60, 79, 129, 135, 138, 149, 159, 168, 171, 220; and John Locke, *Two Treatises of Government,* Peter Laslett, ed. (Cambridge: Cambridge University Press, 1960), First Treatise, §86.

[19] Locke, *Two Treatises of Government,* Second Treatise, §§134-5, 195.

[20] Locke, *Essays on the Law of Nature,* p. 169.

[21] John Locke, "On the Conduct of the Understanding," in John Locke, *The Works of John Locke* (London, 1823), vol. III, §43.

[22] Locke treats natural law as a "decree of the divine will" (Locke, *Essays on the Law of Nature,* pp. 111, 198) and consequently, places himself in the voluntarist Ockhamist theological tradition in assuming that human reason can judge whether the norms of natural law are good or not, but such judgment does not constitute the criterion of their objective validity (See John W. Yolton, *Locke and the Compass of Human Understanding* [Cambridge: Cambridge University Press, 1970], pp. 168-69; Dunn, *Political Thought of John Locke,* pp. 187-99; Merwyn S. Johnson, *Locke on Freedom: An Incisive Study of the Thought of John Locke* [Austin: Best Print Co., 1977], pp. 23-45. For an opposite point of view, see Wolfgang von Leyden, "Introduction" in John Locke, *Essays on the Law of Nature,* Wolfgang von Leyden, ed. [Oxford: Clarendon Press, 1954], pp. 57-58. Despite some deviations from this position [see Locke, *Two Treatises of Government,* Second Treatise, §195], Locke never worked out any alternative to it [Compare John Colman, *John Locke's Moral Philosophy* (Edinburgh: Edinburgh University Press, 1983), p. 48.])

[23] Locke stresses this point in a comment on Hobbes: "An Hobbist, with his

principle of self-preservation, whereof himself is to be judge, will not easily admit a great many plain duties of morality," Peter King, *The Life of John Locke, with Extracts from his Correspondence, Journals and Commonplace Books* (London, 1830), vol. I, p. 191.

[24] Dunn, *Political Thought of John Locke*, p. 79.
[25] Locke, *Two Treatises of Government*, Second Treatise, §7.
[26] Ibid., §§129-30.
[27] Ibid., §67.
[28] Ibid., §§52-69, 170.
[29] Ibid., §19.
[30] Ibid., §16.
[31] Ibid., §6, 129-130, 171.
[32] Ibid., §192.

[33] Locke refers to the first variety of the state of nature in §19 of the Second Treatise and indicates that this "is properly the State of Nature." The second variety, "the ordinary state of nature," he describes in §91 of the Second Treatise. Although the content of this concept differs in both thinkers, Locke's normative state of nature proper corresponds with Pufendorf's normative *status naturalis in ordine singulorum hominum ad se ipsos,* and Locke's empirical ordinary state of nature corresponds with Pufendorf's empirical *status naturalis in ordine ad alios homines.* (See Samuel Pufendorf, *De Officio Hominis et Civis juxta legem naturalem libri duo* [New York: Oxford University Press,1927], 2.1.2., and Samuel Pufendorf, *De Jure Nature et Gentium libri Octo 1688,* Latin and English edition, 2 vols, translated by C.H. Oldfather and W.A. Oldfather [Oxford: Clarendon Press, 1934], 2.2.1. For further discussion of this issue, see Leonard Krieger, *The Politics of Discretion* [Chicago and London: The University of Chicago Press, 1965], pp. 89-101, and Hans Medick, *Naturzustand und Naturgeschichte der buergerlichen Gesellschaft* [Goettingen: Sourkamp, 1973], pp. 40-63.)

[34] Although sometimes Locke tries—contradicting his own strategy—to prove the historicity of the state of nature proper—a condition that rules out the existence of any government. He insists that there are "plain instances" and "manifest footsteps" of *"People free and in the State of Nature,* that being met together incorporated and *began a Common-wealth"* (Locke, *Two Treatises of Government,* Second Treatise, §103). Whoever denies these claims shows "a strange inclination to deny [the] evident matter of fact" that the beginning of civil society was accomplished "by the uniting together of several Men [previously] free and independent one of another" (Locke, *Two Treatises of Government,* Second Treatise, §102). Making use of his impressive anthropological knowledge based upon the travellers' reports of his time, Locke supports his position with "manifest proofs," referring to America (that is, to Brazil, Florida, and Peru) where, he claims, there was "no Government at all," since men there "for a long time had neither Kings nor Commonwealths" (Locke, *Two*

Treatises of Government, Second Treatise, §102). Other proofs are derived from the Bible and concern the peoples described in Genesis; Locke writes: "we know not who were their Governors, nor what their Form of Government, but only that they were divided into little Independent Societies, speaking different Languages" (Locke, *Two Treatises of Government*, First Treatise, §144). Yet, as Martin Seliger rightly points out, such proofs miss their aim: they do not contain true examples of the governmentless state of nature proper (Martin Seliger, *Liberal Politics of John Locke* [New York: Praeger 1968], pp. 85-88). For example, Locke refers to communities that *"lived in Troops,"* and were "divided into little Independent Societies," choosing their kings like "the *Kings* of the *Indians* in *America*." He also adds that they had their judges, generals and governors. Elsewhere he describes the same communities as elective monarchies—that is, as one of the forms of commonwealth whose existence, by Locke's own account, unquestionably puts an end to the state of nature. Moreover, Locke admits that "the love, and want of Society" serve to keep people in a community, where "without some Government it would be hard for them to live together," and that, consequently, "Government is hardly to be avoided amongst Men that live together" (Locke, *Two Treatises of Government*, First Treatise §144 and Locke, *Two Treatises of Government*, Second Treatise §§74, 101, 102, 105, 108, 158). In sum, all of Locke's "proofs" refer not to people living in the state of nature proper, but to primitive civil societies (Locke, *Two Treatises of Government*, Second Treatise §102). Locke clearly fails to prove the historicity of his state of nature proper (for an opposing view, see William G. Batz, "The Historical Anthropology of John Locke," *Journal of the History of Ideas*, vol. XXXV, no. 4 [1974]: 663-71).

[35]Locke, *Two Treatises of Government*, Second Treatise, §4.
[36]Ibid., §4.
[37]Aware of the differences in human capacities, Locke writes that people "should" be considered equal (not that they "are"). This has led some scholars to treat Locke's understanding of natural equality as a moral imperative rather than as a statement of fact. See Willmoore Kendall, "John Locke and the Doctrine of Majority Rule," *Illinois Studies in the Social Sciences*, XXVI, no. 2 (1941), pp. 68, 76; Laslett's note in Locke, *Two Treatises of Government*, Second Treatise, §4 and Seliger, *Liberal Politics of John Locke*, p. 50.
[38]Locke, *Two Treatises of Government*, Second Treatise, §54.
[39]Ibid., §4.
[40]Ibid., §22.
[41]When Locke writes on the "Law of Reason" (Locke, *Two Treatises of Government*, First Treatise, §101; Locke, *Two Treatises of Government*, Second Treatise, §57) he means the law of nature discovered—not created—by reason. See Johnson's dispute with Laslett in Johnson, *Locke on Freedom*, p. 94.
[42]Second Treatise, §54-57.
[43]Locke, *Essay concerning Human Understanding*, 2.21.67.

⁴⁴Locke, *Two Treatises of Government,* Second Treatise, §57. For Locke's concept of freedom see ch. 4, sec. II below.
⁴⁵Locke, *Two Treatises of Government,* Second Treatise, §24.
⁴⁶Ibid., §16.
⁴⁷Ibid., §24.
⁴⁸Ibid., §23.
⁴⁹Ibid., §6.
⁵⁰Ibid., §23.
⁵¹Ibid., §54.
⁵²Ibid., §55.
⁵³Ibid., §123.
⁵⁴Ibid., §56.
⁵⁵Ibid., §123, 61.
⁵⁶Ibid., §172.
⁵⁷Ibid., §60.
⁵⁸For a discussion of the postulate of intellectual self-reliance as a leitmotif in Locke's works, see Geraint Parry, *John Locke* (London: George Allen & Unwin, 1978), pp. 42-49. Compare also the highly ideological treatment of this issue by Neal Wood, *The Politics of Locke's Philosophy: A Social Study of An Essay Concerning Human Understanding,* (Berkeley: University of California Press, 1983).
⁵⁹Locke, *Essays on the Law of Nature,* p. 203.
⁶⁰Locke, *The Reasonableness of Christianity,* p. 76.
⁶¹Locke, *Essay concerning Human Understanding,* 4.20.11.
⁶²Locke, *Two Treatises of Government,* Second Treatise, §94.
⁶³Locke, *Essay concerning Human Understanding,* 4.19.14.
⁶⁴Locke, "On the Conduct of the Understanding," §24.
⁶⁵Locke, *Essays on the Law of Nature,* p. 135.
⁶⁶Locke, *Essay concerning Human Understanding,* 4.20.6.
⁶⁷Locke, *Two Treatises of Government,* Second Treatise, §19.
⁶⁸Ibid., §6.
⁶⁹Ibid., §57.
⁷⁰Locke, *Two Treatises of Government,* Second Treatise, §123.
⁷¹In Locke's *Journal,* March 20, 1678, quoted in Richard Ashcraft's "Locke's State of Nature: Historical Fact or Moral Fiction?" *American Political Science Review,* vol. LXII (1968): 907.
⁷²Locke, *Two Treatises of Government,* Second Treatise, §19.
⁷³Ibid., §131.
⁷⁴Ibid., §14.
⁷⁵Ibid., §14.
⁷⁶See John Anglim, "On Locke's State of Nature," *Political Studies,* XXVI, (1978): 78-90.
⁷⁷Locke, *Two Treatises of Government,* Second Treatise, §14.

[78] Compare Robert A. Goldwin, "Locke's State of Nature in Political Society," *Western Political Quarterly,* XXIX, (1976): 126-136.
[79] Locke, *Two Treatises of Government,* Second Treatise, §90.
[80] Dunn, *Political Thought of John Locke,* pp. 99, 101, 103-105, 112-114.
[81] Leo Strauss, *Natural Right and History* (Chicago: The University of Chicago Press, 1953), p. 231; Richard H. Cox, *Locke on War and Peace* (Oxford: Clarendon Press, 1960), p. 45; Robert A. Goldwin, "John Locke," in Leo Strauss and Joseph Cropsey, eds., *History of Political Philosophy* (Chicago: Rand McNally and Company, 1963), pp. 434-442.
[82] Seliger, *Liberal Politics of John Locke,* p. 82; Dunn, *Political Thought of John Locke,* p. 96.
[83] Richard Ashcraft, "Locke's State of Nature: Historical Factor or Moral Fiction?" p. 906. The only author who treats this distinction as the framework of the Lockean categories is Medick, *Naturzustand und Naturgeschichte,* pp. 102-108.

Chapter 3

Power and Property

Having discussed how Filmer and Locke presented the standards of rationality of paternal power or superhuman agency (H[1]) and individual or human agency (C[1]) in their holistic and contractarian models, we can now advance to analyze how each thinker applied these standards to the particular issue of property. For Filmer, property was a part of the social context reflecting the standards of rationality of paternal power, not a result of any effort on the part of individuals. For Locke, property was a result of particular undertakings by individual agents following their own standards of rationality.

To expand on this point, in this chapter I shall present the relations between power and property in both Filmer's and Locke's models. I shall argue that in Filmer's holistic model, the two institutions are inseparable, both in origin and political practice. In disarming Filmer's position Locke introduces a rigorous separation between power and property. He bases his position on his claim that these institutions have different origins and purposes in the state of nature and civil society.

Filmer considers "the grounds of dominion and property" to be "the main principles of government."[1] The unity of power and ownership is an essential attribute of any structure embracing human beings; as such, their conceptual origin can be traced back to "the natural and private dominion of Adam,"[2] the first holder of paternal power. Challenging the proposition that political and economic power differed from each other, Filmer writes:

> I know not what he [Suarez] means by this... *economical power*, nor how or in what it doth really and essentially differ from political. If Adam did or might exercise in his family the same jurisdiction which a King doth now in a commonwealth, then the kinds of power are not distinct. And though they may receive an accidental difference by the amplitude or extent of the bounds of the one beyond the other, yet since the like difference is also found in political estates, it follows that the economical and political power differ no otherwise than a little commonwealth differs from a great one.[3]

This perfect unity of power and property determines the status of the Filmerian man, whose dependence upon his magistrate can be conceived not only in terms of the relation between subject and ruler, but also in terms of the relation between an object of property and a property owner. Filmer leaves no room for doubt that, with respect to this second relation, there can be no difference between persons and goods. As he puts it:

> Adam was the Father, King and Lord over his family: a son, a subject and a servant or a slave, were one and the same thing at first; the Father had power to dispose, or sell his children or servants; whence we find, that at the first reckoning up of goods in scripture, the manservant, and the maidservant are numbered among the possessions and substance of the owner, as other goods were. As for the names of subject, slave, and tyrant, they are not found in the scripture, but what we now call a subject or a slave, is there named no other than a servant.[4]

The unity of power and ownership also means that people, as objects of property, cannot gain property by their own efforts; similarly, as subjects of power, they cannot acquire any power through their own activity. The privilege of both power and property can only be granted to them "from the grace and bounty of Princes."[5] However, in this case, though people enjoy the property with which they are provided, and exercise whatever power is bestowed upon them, they remain themselves objects of property and subjects of power.

The reason for Filmer's denial of any distinction between power and property is fairly clear. If paternal power is to be what Filmer wants it to be, namely, the only cause of all human relations, it must include property; without this, paternal power could play no such role. If property is separated from power, it would deprive power of the character which Filmer ascribes to it.

Comparing Filmer's position to that of his contemporary royalist writers illustrates the degree to which he remained true to his premises. The royalists agreed with him that the origin of property was to be found in the monarch's grant to his subjects. Yet they believed this grant to be irrevocable in political practice, since the subjects' entitlement to property so obtained was sanctioned by custom.[6] Had Filmer conceded this, not only would his paternal power be limited by the customary status of the subjects' property, it would cease to be the only source of all human relations. If subjects could dispose of their property within the limits outlined by custom, free from royal interference, the circulation of property among them would create relations independent of those arranged for them by paternal power. Under such conditions, Filmer's holistic model of social relations could not stand.

Taking aim at his adversary's position on property, Locke begins with the general claim that power and property have different origins and serve different purposes. "Property, whose Original is from the Right a Man has... for the Subsistence and Comfort of his Life, is for the benefit and sole Advantage of the Proprietor," while power exists "for the Preservation of every Man's Right and Property, by preserving him from the Violence or Injury of others, [and so] is for the good of the Governed."[7] Locke rejects Filmer's claim that the exercise of power (in the case of rulers), or the grants of rulers (in the case of their subjects) are entitlements to property; rather, he claims, there are three natural law entitlements to property: labor, inheritance, and charity. He refutes Filmer's claim that people who are under the rule of others are objects of their property and, in discussing the regulation of property in civil society, he defends the separation of political power from the property of its members. But before discussing these issues further, Locke's natural law concept of property needs to be discussed, since he leans on it heavily in explaining his position on property.

Locke's theory of property begins to take shape in the *First Treatise*, where he introduces the concept of inclusive rights,[8] the origin of which he traces to God's grant to the First Parents, as described in Genesis. This grant serves as Locke's theological premise and point of departure for his natural law discussion of property.[9] He uses this reading of Genesis to refute Filmer's argument, which is based upon Adam's right of "Private Domination over the Earth, and all inferior or irrational Creatures."[10] Locke distinguishes property from domination,[11] writing that what God granted to Adam was "not *Private Domination* over the Inferior Creatures, but right in common with all Mankind" in "account of the Property here given him."[12]

Accordingly, Locke's concept of natural property differs from Filmer's because it is a right possessed by all men—a right of use only, not of abuse or alienation.[13] It is a common property, not a private one; it is a right to one's due rather than to one's own. And finally, it is a right that has a specified end, not determined by the proprietor's unbounded will but rather based upon the relation between man and God. It is this relation that gives rational confirmation to the normative character of Locke's concept of common property; the preservation of mankind is the fundamental law of nature,[14] and people "being once born have a right to their Preservation."[15] They are thus entitled not only to defend themselves against the arbitrary acts of others,[16] but to have "Meat and Drink, and such other things, as Nature affords for their Subsistence."[17]

Locke then shifts his discussion from inclusive to exclusive rights. Reason indicates, he argues, that men should "make use of" things belonging to common property "for the Support and Comfort of their being."[18] Therefore, since the world was given to men, "there must of necessity be a means *to appropriate* them some way or other before they can be of any use, or at all beneficial to any particular Man."[19]

The coexistence of these two sorts of rights, inclusive (a "right to") and exclusive (a "right in") is possible because of the fundamental distinction Locke draws between "man" and "person."[20] Man as such, as God's workmanship and property, has an inclusive right to the world in common with others.[21] Man as a person has an exclusive right—a right in his person: he is a proprietor of his person and his actions, and therefore "no Man but he can have a right to what that is once joyned to."[22] Man enjoys the status of a person when he can exercise his own reason,[23] and therefore when he is free.[24] As Locke states in the *Essay concerning Human Understanding*, a person "is a thinking intelligent Being" only if he has "reason and reflection, and can consider it self as it self, the same thinking thing in different times and places; which it does only by that consciousness, which is inseparable from thinking, and as it seems to me essential to it."[25] A person is therefore an individual capable of performing intentional, deliberate actions,[26] of shaping his own personality. "This personality extends it *self* beyond present Existence to what is past, only by consciousness, whereby it becomes concerned and accountable, owns and imputes to it *self* past Actions, just upon the same ground, and for the same reason, that it does the present."[27] Accordingly, the criterion for ownership of action comes into being once these conscious, deliberate actions have been performed.[28]

Locke's understanding of property, including both inclusive and exclusive rights, corresponds to the concept that Latin authors in the seventeenth century described by using the term *suum*, that is, a sphere that must not be violated.[29] Given the theological origin of this sphere, for Locke property is a deeply moral concept, one that encompasses not only a person's goods and possessions, but also his actions, liberty, life, and body.[30] With Locke's natural law concept of property outlined above, I can now proceed to discuss how Locke develops this concept into an attack on and alternative to Filmer's concept of property.

First, the issue of entitlement. For Filmer, entitlement emerges from the power exercised by rulers; for Locke entitlement comes from labor, inheritance, and charity. Entitlement to property through labor permits the Lockean man to exclude "the common right of other men." Whatever man "removes out of the State that Nature hath provided, and left it in, he hath mixed his *Labour* with, and joyned to it something that is his own, and thereby makes it his *Property*."[31] Locke applies his concept of appropriation to the spontaneous products of nature, to animals, and to land. He states that picking up acorns with the intention of keeping them for oneself must be sufficient to make them one's own, because in this way one "added something to them more than Nature... had done,"[32] and one "had thereby *Property* in them."[33] The other examples—killing a deer, catching a fish, or taking up ambergris in the ocean—are of a similar kind, because the animals and products become one's own goods suitable for use.[34] Turning to the "chief matter of property," the land itself, Locke maintains that property in land is acquired in the same way, that is, by "annexing" it to something of one's own—one's labor.[35] The laborer may justly call two effects of his action his own: the reconstituted wasteland[36] (the earth itself remains the property of God, who provides man with land in "waste," that is, in a wild state, for his use[37]); and the products of his tilling, planting, and cultivating.[38] While the laborer's action is unquestionably an extension of his personality to the appropriated objects—"something of the spiritual ego is infused into the object"[39]—it is more than that, since the mere extension of ego could justify Filmer's thesis that children are the property of their parents.[40] Accordingly, the essence of extending one's personality is that intentional acts change material into useful goods and thereby make them one's own.[41] Intentional creative activity is the act of a maker, based upon that maker's knowledge, which includes the cause and effect of his work.[42]

As a permanent component of the efforts taken to preserve mankind, appropriation is legitimized and governed by natural law. Locke writes, "the same Law of Nature, that does by this means give us Property, does also *bound* that *Property* too."[43] In other words, the provisions of natural law prevent individual appropriation which could cause injury to others. Despite the fact that "God gave the world richly for mankind to enjoy," it is not permissible for anyone to take more than he can consume. Appropriation is justifiable only when it contributes to the preservation of mankind: "As much as any one can make use of to any advantage of life before it spoils; so much he may, by his labor, fix a property in," that is, "within the *bounds*, set by reason of what might serve for his *use*."[44] This restriction is imposed upon every kind of object that might be appropriated, movables as well as the land itself.[45] Anyone who allows things to spoil "in his Possession without their due use" commits an offense against "the common Law of Nature"[46] and must expect two consequences: he can be punished for the invasion of his Neighbours' sphere, or he can be deprived of his property in land, which, in spite of enclosure, "must be looked on as Waste."[47]

Because he thought it important to make very clear the process of appropriation, Locke places it in the idyllic harmony of the state of nature proper. Only in this way can he describe the perfect operation of all natural law limits on appropriation as well as on man's natural right to the means of preservation. Accordingly, Locke does not extend the limits on appropriation beyond those set by one's needs, and he lays down the proviso that appropriation must leave enough and as good for others.[48]

In addition to its moral aspect, this proviso is of great tactical significance for Locke's polemic against Filmer. In his attack on Grotius, Filmer indicates two vulnerable elements of negative community (where property is not held in common but in distinct portions and various manners), which were later repeated by Pufendorf.[49] Filmer writes:

> Certainly it was a rare felicity, that all men in the world at one instant of time should agree together in one mind to change the natural community of all things into private dominion: for without such a unanimous consent it was not possible for community to be altered: for if but one man in the world had dissented, the alteration had been unjust, because that man by the law of nature had a right to the common use of all things in the world; so that to have given a propriety of any one thing to any other, had been to have robbed him of his right to the common use of all things.[50]

Locke, stating his argument in terms of positive community (where property is held in common by everyone in the same manner), manages to avoid both these objections. First, he points out that the objection concerning robbery is not relevant to his solution. Discussing the acorn-gathering example, he asks: "will any one say he had no right to those Acorns or Apples he thus appropriated, because he had not the consent of all Mankind to make them his? Was it a Robbery thus to assume to himself what belonged to all in Common?"[51] He then points to the early stages of man's history: "Nor was this *appropriation* of any parcel of *Land*, by improving it, any prejudice to any other Man, since there was still enough, and as good left; and more than the yet unprovided could use."[52] It is therefore possible for an individual to appropriate as much as is required for the support of his life, without any reduction of common property to property in several. Second, Locke indicates that any consideration of the express consent of all fellow commoners that might prevent them from robbing one another of their property would have been pointless and would inevitably have created obstacles to the performance of the natural duty of preservation.[53] As he explains, referring to the convention of the English common[54] and to the example of water running in a fountain,[55] common property remains common and there can be "no doubt of Right, no room for quarrel."[56]

Locke's two other natural entitlements to individual ownership, inheritance and charity, are natural obligations drawn from property relations. In the case of the family, the divinely imposed duty to preserve mankind takes the form of a duty toward the "continuation of Species."[57] When it conforms to this end, the family is a positive community, a "community of Goods, and the Power over them, mutual Assistance, and Maintenance."[58] Accordingly, contrary to Filmer,[59] Locke leaves no room for the father's individual right to property. Children are not required to obtain his consent to individuate familial goods,[60] which come "to be wholly theirs, when death having put an end to their Parents use of it, hath taken them from their Possessions and this we call Inheritance."[61] The only alternative to inheritance is the reversion of the familial goods to the community.[62]

Although Locke never doubted that labor is the most suitable means for a person to perform the duty to preserve mankind—"Justice gives every Man a Title to the product of his honest Industry"—he added that it must be coordinated with charity,[63] which "gives every Man a Title to so much out of another's Plenty, as will keep him from extream want, where he has no means to subsist otherwise."[64] Locke treats charity as a duty on the part of the wealthy.[65] While he nowhere gives any sustained analysis of the duty of charity, it seems safe to assume that he understands it as more than the mere duty not to deliberately permit other men to die. Many times he expresses the opinion that the needy man, who cannot work, is entitled to lead a comfortable life:[66] "every one must have meat, drink, clothing, and firing. So much goes out of the stock of the kingdom, whether they work or not."[67]

With his three natural entitlements to property—labor, inheritance, and charity—which together make up his concept of natural justice, Locke denies Filmer's claims that only power can justify ownership. He then rejects his adversary's pronouncement that people who are under the rule of others are the property of their rulers. Locke's discussion of this issue can be divided into two parts: the first contains a rejection of Filmer's claim that subjects are the property of their rulers; the second denies Filmer's insistence that servants are owned by their masters.

The first point is traced back to the natural equality of all human beings in their moral status as God's property. The Lockean man cannot be an object of property, neither as understood by Filmer, that is, an object of abuse and alienation, nor as defined by Locke, who regarded property as a means to preserve others. Though "inferior creatures" are objects of property, people were never "made as so many Herds of Cattle, only for Service, Use, and Pleasure of their Princes."[68]

Locke discusses the second point, that of the master-servant relationship, in terms of the social division of labor, which is one of the conventional obligations within the state of nature proper.[69] Locke does not deny the patriarchal element in the servant's position; rather, he admits that a servant living temporarily in his master's family has to conform himself to its "domestic rule" and "ordinary discipline," that is, to the family power of his master.[70] Nevertheless, as a free man the Lockean servant—contrary to Filmer's position—cannot be anybody's property. Moreover, he himself is "capable of Property." Hence, it is not paternal power that gives the master the title to his servant's service; rather, it is the contract by which the servant voluntarily sells his master "the Service he undertakes to do in exchange for Wages he is to receive."[71]

Unlike in his other writings, in the *Two Treatises* Locke's consideration of the relations of subjects and rulers and of servants and masters leaves no room for the use of power as a tool to increase property. Indeed, in this discourse the rigorous distinction between power and property excludes, for example, any possibility of a ruler's enrichment by imposing compulsory labor upon those over whom he exercises his power.

The Marxist interpretation of Locke's concept of property is an influential one in contemporary scholarship that yields conclusions that are fundamentally opposed to those reached above. I will thus bring this interpretation into our discussion so that, in addition to having it serve as a contrast to my own, I can address the conclusions that it reaches.

Regarding Locke's social division of labor, according to the Marxist interpretation the master-servant relation expresses, above all, economic compulsion and the alienation of labor. The commentaries of C.B.

Power and Property 51

Macpherson and his followers are model examples of this alienation of labor interpretation. Take for example their comments on the following passage, in which Locke indicates how labor creates a right in its product without the consent of other commoners:

> Thus the Grass my Horse has bit; the Turfs my Servant has cut; and the Ore I have digg'd in any place where I have a right to them in common with others, become my *Property*, without the assignment or consent of any body. The *labour* that was mine, removing them out of that common state they were in, hath *fixed* my *Property* in them[72]

In the Marxist interpretation, this passage is treated as proof that Locke's theory of property "is not at all inconsistent with the assumption of a natural right to alienate one's labor in return for a wage," and thus confirms the bourgeois character of Locke's whole concept of property, according to which property establishes "a right to dispose of, to exchange, to alienate."[73]

This notion of the alienation of labor that is attributed to Locke is further supported, it is said, by ascribing a compulsory character to labor as it is described in the *Two Treatises*. Such a reading is based upon the conviction that, after the introduction of money into the state of nature, when there was no longer plenty of land left for appropriation, the only way in which those without land could satisfy their natural right to subsistence was by their labor.[74] Therefore, it is argued, the Lockean idea of natural order is the perfect model of capitalist society, in which individuals are free from legal restraints but obliged to conform themselves to rules dictated by market forces. It is then concluded that Locke's intention, already expressed in his discussion of the state of nature, was to justify full economic control by the class of property owners over the class of "the propertyless" (their term, which ignores Locke's claim that man has property in himself and thus cannot be "propertyless")—a control that would approximate political power.

If this reading of Locke is accurate, then in his consideration of property he must have been dedicated, not to the division of power and ownership, but rather to their unity. The conclusion that emerges from this interpretation is that the only difference between Filmer and Locke on this issue, is that the former treated power as the title to property and the latter treated property as the title to power.

However, the text and historical context of the *Two Treatises* provide ample evidence that casts doubt on this interpretation. First, the wage relationship. As has been shown above, labor is understood by Locke to be the laborer's creative act, performed in accordance with his will; accordingly, "We cannot alienate any part of our personalities, but we can alienate that with which we have chosen to mix our personalities."[75] Therefore, the servant cannot sell his labor in return for a wage, but only the product of his laboring over a specific period of service in the household of his master. It is true that Locke writes of "the labour that was mine," but when he discusses the wage relationship he uses the word "service," not "labour."[76] Thus, in spite of his inconsistent use of terminology, the passage cited above cannot be treated as a conceptual alternative to Locke's precisely stated notion of the wage relationship. He never developed such an alternative.

Also, in discussing the wage relationship, Locke clearly refers not to capitalist manufacture, which appears well after his time, but to the dominant working unit in pre-industrial Stuart England—the household.[77] Thus, it is the character of that working unit that should provide the basis for interpreting the "Turfs" passage.[78] No society before industrialization systematically subdivided the work of each productive specialty into the limited operations found in capitalist manufacture; and it was in manufacture rather than in the household that a capitalist bought "not an agreed amount of labor, but the power to labor over an agreed period of time."[79] Locke does not refer to the division of labor into specialized operations in manufacturing, but to the distribution of tasks, crafts, or specialties of production.[80] Accordingly, the average servant or day laborer[81] in Locke's time (and, hence, the Lockean servant), was told what to do but not how to do it,[82] that is, he was able, because of his technical knowledge, to perform creative work in accordance with his will.[83]

Now to address the second claim, that Locke intended to justify power for the class of property owners over the class of the "propertyless," thus creating the perfect model of "capitalist society." While this interpretation may prove extremely satisfying to its authors in ideological terms, it is at odds with Locke's attitude to the social reality of his day and, importantly, with the text of the *Two Treatises*.

To begin, if Locke had been an advocate of the "spirit of capitalism" and economic compulsion, as Macpherson believes he was, then in order to increase the economic pressure upon the poor to establish their direct dependency upon the rich, Locke should have argued for the abolition of all sources of subsistence that did not result from their labor. In reality, however, Locke did exactly the opposite. For example, he asserts that the rich have duty of charity towards the poor. But it is Locke's rejection of Filmer's unity of power and property that is the strongest and most direct proof of the groundlessness of the Marxist claim that Locke treats property as a title to power. Locke emphasizes most passionately that it is impossible "that he that is Proprietor of the whole World may deny all the rest of Mankind Food, and so at his pleasure starve them, if they do not acknowledge his Sovereignty, and Obey his Will." This is impossible since, as Locke stresses, it is wrong to assume "that Property in Land gives a Man Power over the Life of another."[84]

Locke's separation of power and property, which has thus far been presented in the harmony of the state of nature proper, is confirmed by the manner in which he discusses property in civil society. In this imperfect condition, Locke is faced with a complication—money—which he believed to be the greatest challenge to the separation of power and ownership, since it changes economic (and thus moral) relations.

The acceptance of money as a store of wealth and a means of exchange is the most important conventional arrangement in Locke's consideration of property.[85] Money, according to Locke, was introduced to continue the practice of hoarding useless but permanent things, which man exchanged for the products of his labor. In this way, since he could "keep those by him all his Life, he invaded not the Right of others."[86] Locke's account of money as an outgrowth of barter is traditionally Aristotelian, especially when he admits that its invention brought about the unnatural desire to accumulate more than is necessary.[87] The direct consequence of this psychological need was a general increase in holdings[88] and acceleration of the movement toward unequal holdings (even though these holdings did not themselves create inequality).[89] These were the only changes that the invention of money brought into economic relations, since "the intrinsick value of things" did not change and still depended "only on their usefulness to the Life of Man"[90] and not on money. It is still labor that makes the greatest part of the value of things man enjoys,[91] and labor that created useful goods for the support of life and for convenience both before and after the introduction of money.[92] Indeed, Locke writes that it is the necessity of meeting these natural needs, and not the invention of money, that is the original source of socioeconomic growth.[93]

Since the circulation of money and the social consequences carried with it are empirical facts, they are subject to moral judgment according to the principles of natural law. Thus, Locke's rigorously underscored distinction between useful things ("goods," "good things," "things really useful")[94] and other things whose value is only granted by human agreement is an expression of his negative evaluation of money. This moral disapproval is directed at the shift in the source of human motivation caused by the appearance of money, a shift from need and convenience to the desire for more than is needed. Nevertheless, Locke indicates that this most corrupt of human motives[95] is not sufficient to alter the principles of natural law, and that God gave the world "to the use of the Industrious and Rational (and *Labour* was to be *his Title* to it) not to the Fancy or Covetousness of the Quarrelsom and Contentious."[96]

Accordingly, it is hard to believe, as do prominent Marxist scholars,[97] that Locke regards unlimited appropriation as the essence of rationality. Though the circulation of money leads to an increase in appropriation, Locke does not conclude that rationality is more prevalent after its introduction than before. On the contrary, he believes that craving for more than is needed is irrational, and motivated by "*amor sceleratus habendi*, evil Concupiscence,"[98] which alters people's estimation of the value of things. Locke thus treated unlimited appropriation as a morally perilous endeavor,[99] which, if one insists on calling it "rational," was so only in an expedient sense, in that cleverness was used to circumvent the natural limitations on acquisitiveness commanded by the law of nature.[100]

After money was accepted by the tacit consent of mankind, the individualization of property lost its previous moral dimension, a dimension it had in the natural order. Since appropriation did not require consent from fellow commoners, an increase in private holdings of land became a source of frequent conflict that prevented some people from exercising their natural right to acquire property, especially land. Consequently, even though God gave the world to men in common,[101] the law of nature, which orders the preservation of mankind, could not be carried out.[102]

These conditions could be improved only because of Locke's separation of power and ownership. Indeed, when the institution of property ceases to benefit the community and becomes a means for some members to prevent others from enjoying their property rights, the task of political power is to set up conventional rules that restore the previous moral status of property as a means toward preserving mankind. These rules are positive laws within civil society:[103] "Obligations of the Law of Nature cease not in Society, but only in many Cases are drawn closer, and have by Humane Laws known Penalities annexed to them, to inforce their observation."[104] Therefore, in civil society the imperative to preserve mankind takes the form of the public good—the conventional goal of political power.[105] The law of nature calls for the preservation of each man[106] and political power in civil society "can have no other *end or measure*... but to preserve the Members of that Society in their Lives, Liberties and Possessions."[107]

Power and Property

The Lockean man enters "into Society with others for the securing and regulating of Property,"[108] exchanging his natural rights for conventionally defined ones. The conceptual background of this solution is that positive laws made by civil society reach back to the natural power of each of its members to do "*whatsoever he thought fit for the Preservation of himself, and the rest of Mankind.*"[109] The member of civil society is "in a new State, wherein he is to enjoy many Conveniencies, from the labor, assistance, and society of others in the same Community, as well as protection from its whole strength; he is to part also with as much of his natural liberty in providing for himself, as the good, prosperity, and safety of the Society shall require."[110] Accordingly, he submits all his possessions, including land,[111] to the rule of civil society, which determines their status by positive law.[112] By civil society's norms, "every one may know what is his."[113]

The question often raised in scholarship is that of the extent and character of the regulation of property introduced and carried out by civil society. Given his natural law presentation of property, which includes both the individualistic self-ownership argument and its Thomist background implying traditional social obligations, Locke's position on these regulations is far from unequivocal. There is no doubt that his argument for natural self-ownership results in his describing the task of political power in civil society as only the "Regulating and Preserving of Property."[114] However, it is also true that his rich discussion of natural justice, which implies that charity is the natural duty of the wealthy, opens the door to an interpretation that ascribes a distributive principle to civil society.[115] As most scholars acknowledge, there is no room in Locke for a reconciliation of these two solutions.[116]

The only route available in determining Locke's position is an indirect one: examining and contrasting his discussion of each solution. In almost every chapter of the *Second Treatise* Locke takes pains to construct a highly complex mechanism for regulating, preserving, and enforcing natural property rights, including the act of social contract, the creation of civil society and civil government with all its agencies and, as a last resort, the institution of resistance. However, he does not provide any comparable mechanism for regulating, preserving, and executing natural duties such as, for example, indicating ways of transferring possessions from one of civil society's members to another, which would enforce the natural social obligations he discusses. It is thus difficult to escape the conclusion that the case for property regulation that would lead to distributive justice in Locke's civil society, although conceptually admissible, cannot be based upon any solid textual evidence.[117]

Even if one finds this conclusion unconvincing, it will not affect the broader conclusion, namely, that power and property belong to the normative part of Locke's doctrine. As such, they serve man and his preservation. However, this service depends on the rigid, permanent separation of power and property. It is this separation that enables the Lockean man to use power and property for his end and not be turned into a subject of power and an object of property (as is his Filmerian counterpart), because, separated, each institution limits the other. In Locke, property restricts power and power regulates property.

Those who hold political power in civil society cannot deprive its members of property without their consent,[118] but it is the political power that regulates the property of civil society's members in order to maintain relations that preserve mankind. Thus, contrary to Macpherson's interpretation,[119] there is no more room in Locke for absolute property than there is for absolute power. As is the case with absolute power, for Locke to have accepted absolute property would have meant approving Filmer's holistic assumption of the unity of power and ownership, which would have rendered impossible the preservation of mankind. Absolute power would have meant the ownership of subjects and their goods, just as absolute property would have given the propertied man power over "the propertyless."

In Locke, property rights are always regulated and enforced by rules and institutional arrangements. In the state of nature, they are regulated by the law of nature and enforced by the two natural powers of the individuals; in civil society, they are regulated by the positive law stated by the legislative and enforced by the policies of the executive. Thus, the property rights of some can never extend to the point that they would undermine Locke's very normative system that protects the rights to life, liberty, and the estate of others. To argue, as does Macpherson, that Locke treats property so as to encourage the ruling minority to increase their wealth and privileges at the expense of the rest of the population, is every bit as ill-founded as taking Locke's treatment of power as a justification of (for example), royal force and robbery.

Summary

My goal in this chapter was to outline the relationships between power and property in Filmer and Locke. Filmer offered an absolute unity of these institutions while Locke insisted upon their separation. Locke rejected Filmer's claims that the origin of property was to be found in paternal power and that subjects were therefore the objects of their rulers' property. He specified—in the setting of his state of nature—three natural law entitlements to property that were independent of any sort of power: labor, inheritance, and charity. Similarly, discussing the implementation of natural law in civil society, he indicated the principal separation of political power from the property of its members.

That Locke's discussion of property is an integral part of his controversy with Filmer is not always sufficiently stressed in scholarship.[120] For example, in Tully's study, Filmer is treated only as one of Locke's many adversaries, and not as the one against whom his presentation of property was aimed.[121] There are several possible explanations for this: First, most sequences of Locke's discussion of property were presented in more precise language and more sophisticated theoretical constructions than the rest of his refutation of Filmerism. Second, the reason for the relatively weak connection between Locke's discussion of property and the rest of his polemic with Filmer was that Locke treated property as a natural law institution and discussed it in the strictly scholarly terms developed by the respectable natural law theorists of his century. Indeed, given that he had to modify some of their premises in order to avoid any rationalistic justification of absolutism within the natural law framework,[122] Locke's presentation sometimes gives the impression that it was aimed no less against these pro-absolutist elements among his fellow natural law theorists than against Filmerism. Third, because the issue of property is still the most ideologically sensitive part of Locke studies, scholars sometimes allow themselves to be excessively influenced by their own political objectives, leading them to miss and Locke's objectives in attacking Filmerism. This is especially true of Marxist authors—such as Macpherson and Wood—who impute to Locke certain categories of social thought the character of which is profoundly nineteenth century.[123] If, as these authors write, Locke's main task in the *Two Treatises* is understood to be the proclamation of the coming of capitalism, it is difficult for them to take his highly sophisticated and painstaking discussion of property simply as a sequence of his political polemic with Filmer.

---

[1]Robert Filmer, "Observations upon Aristotle's Politics," in Robert Filmer, *Patriarcha and Other Political Works of Sir Robert Filmer,* Peter Laslett, ed. (Oxford: Basil Blackwell, 1949), p. 187.

[2] Robert Filmer, "Patriarcha," in Robert Filmer, *Patriarcha and Other Political Works of Sir Robert Filmer,* Peter Laslett, ed. (Oxford: Basil Blackwell, 1949), p. 71.

[3] Ibid., p. 78.

[4] Filmer, "Observations upon Aristotle's Politics," p. 188.

[5] Robert Filmer, "Patriarcha," in Robert Filmer, *Patriarcha and Other Political Works of Sir Robert Filmer,* Peter Laslett, ed. (Oxford: Basil Blackwell, 1949), p. 55.

[6] See Robert Sheringham, *The Kings' Supremacy Asserted* (London, 1660), p. 103 and Sir George Mackenzie, *Jus Regium* (London, 1684), pp. 51-52. Compare James Daly, *Sir Robert Filmer and English Political Thought* (Toronto: Toronto University Press, 1979), pp. 53-54.

[7] John Locke, *Two Treatises of Government,* Peter Laslett, ed. (Cambridge: Cambridge University Press, 1988), First Treatise, §92.

[8] For a discussion of the distinction between common property (understood as inclusive rights "not to be excluded from" or "to be included in") and private property (treated as a right to "exclude others from" plus whatever other specified moral or legal powers over the referent the rightholders may enjoy), see C.B. Macpherson, *Democratic Theory: Essays in Retrieval* (Oxford: Clarendon Press, 1973), pp. 123-125.

[9] In many respects, including this theological point of departure, Locke's concept of property is close to the Thomist tradition, especially to Suarez. Compare St. Thomas Aquinas, *Summa Theologica,* Latin and English edition, 60 vols., T. Gilby, ed. (O.P.London, 1964), II.II.66.2; Francis Suarez, *De legibus ac Deo legislatore, Selections from Three Works,* Latin and English edition, 2 vols., translated by G.L.Williams (Oxford: Clarendon Press, 1944), 2.14.16. For the link between Locke's and Suarez's thought, see "Introduction" in John Locke, *Essays on the Law of Nature,* Wolfgang von Leyden, ed. (Oxford: Clarendon Press, 1954), pp. 36-37 and Quentin Skinner, *The Foundations of Modern Political Thought* (Cambridge: Cambridge University Press, 1978), vol I, pp. 158-59, 163, 165, 174. James Tully uses Suarez's work as an object of comparison to illuminate innovations and continuities in seventeenth century natural law theories (see his *Discourse on Property: John Locke and his Adversaries* [Cambridge: Cambridge University Press, 1980]).

[10] Locke, *Two Treatises of Government,* First Treatise, §24.

[11] Ibid., §§36, 39, 45-47.

[12] Ibid., §24.

[13] Locke's attitude in this case is best captured in his discussion on travel in his *Journal,* where he writes that man should treat the world as a foreign country, using and enjoying what it offers yet leaving everything as it is (see Peter King, *The Life and Letters of John Locke,with Extracts from his Journals and Common-Place Books* [London, 1830], vol. II, p. 92). This attitude is based upon the workmanship model: the world belongs to its Maker and men are only at liberty to use it with his

permission (see First Treatise, §39). Compare Tully, *Discourse on Property,* p. 61.
    [14]John Locke, *Two Treatises of Government,* Peter Laslett, ed. (Cambridge: Cambridge University Press, 1988), Second Treatise, §135.
    [15]Ibid., §25. In his discussion of natural property, when arguing for inclusive rights, Locke gives it a broad moral dimension, which placed him very close to the Thomist tradition but caused an inevitable clash with the seventeenth century natural law authorities—Grotius and Pufendorf.

Aquinas uses the term *dominium* in two ways. Defining the world as God's natural property, he says that God has dominion over its substance. Nevertheless, "dominion" over natural things in the sense of "use" is natural and common to men (Aquinas, *Summa Theologica,* II.II.66.1). He also makes a clear distinction between *proprietas,* understood as individual or exclusive rights, and *communitas rerum,* treated as common property (ibid., II.II.66.2).

Suarez developed Aquinas' distinction into the theory of subjective rights. Rights are to be derived from the concept of justice. Justice in its generic meaning stands for every moral virtue because every virtue is directed toward equity. Accordingly, "right" in its generic sense refers to the general objective of virtue in the abstract. "Justice" in its specific meaning signifies a special virtue which renders to another that which is his due. Consequently, "right" in its specific meaning refers to the equity which is due to each individual as a matter of justice (Suarez, *De legibus ac Deo legislatore,* I.2.4). In turn, Suarez redistributes the objective right in the specific sense into two subjective rights: a right in a thing, *ius in re,* i.e., a claim to that which is already one's own and is possessed, and a right to a thing, *ius ad rem,* a claim to that which belongs to a person in the sense of being his due. Tully stresses the conceptual unity between Suarez's *ius in re* and Locke's "property in," as well as *ius ad rem* and "property to" (Tully, *Discourse on Property,* p. 67). The introduction of *ius ad rem* serves to redistribute common property because, as Suarez writes: "Nature has conferred upon all men in common dominion over all things, and consequently has given every man a power to use those things: but nature has not so conferred private domination" (ibid., 2.14.16).

In turn, the difference between Locke's and Grotius' conceptual origins of property is fundamental. Grotius radically broke with the Thomists" traditional understanding of common property when, anticipating Filmer, he used *dominium* interchangeably with *proprietas* and treated all sorts of property only in terms of exclusive rights (Hugo Grotius, *De Iure Belli ac Pacis* [Oxford: Clarendon Press, 1925], 2.2.1). Although, "God conferred upon the human race a general right in things, *ius in res,* of a lower nature (ibid., 2.2.2.1), common ownership means that each owner has a right over his share, because property is a result of occupation, see Hugo Grotius, *Of the Freedom of the Seas,* translated by Ralph van Deman Magoffin (Oxford: Oxford University Press, 1916), pp. 21-22, 27. What is not or cannot be occupied is still *communia omnia,* i.e., *propria nullius* (ibid., p. 28).

Pufendorf refined Grotius' achievement. He treated property as a right in the substance of a thing and assumed that property (but not possession of a thing) cannot belong in the same manner and in whole to more than one person (Samuel Pufendorf, *De Jure Naturae et Gentium* [Oxford: Clarendon Press, 1934], 4.4.2). Pufendorf admitted that men have a power to use things as any animal has but this "turns into a proper Right, when it creates this moral Effect in other Persons, that they shall not hinder him in the free Use of the Conveniences, and shall themselves forbear to use them without his Consent" (ibid., 3.5.3). Before this introduction of private property by agreement, men are, as in Grotius, in a negative community (ibid., 4.4.2). Conventional private property or private domination is even sanctioned by God (ibid., 4.4.4). In sum, Grotius and Pufendorf, dissolving the distinction between "right in" and "right to," committed a theoretical simplification of great doctrinal significance. They deprived property of its previous status as a natural law institution and reduced it to an instrument of governing.

[16]Locke, *Two Treatises of Government,* Second Treatise, §§13, 35.

[17]Ibid., §25.

[18]Ibid, §§26, 34.

[19]Ibid., §26. Nevertheless, contrary to the position taken by Grotius and Pufendorf, this does not entail a dissolution of the positive community, because an agent with an exclusive right still remains "a Tenant in common." Ibid., §26, see also Tully, *Discourse on Property,* p. 105.

[20]In using the term "person," Locke evidently follows Aquinas, who defined person as a master of his action through his will. See Aquinas, *Summa Theologica,* I.II.2.11. Compare also Suarez, *De legibus ac Deo Legislatore,* 2.14.16.

[21]Locke, *Two Treatises of Government,* Second Treatise, §27.

[22]Ibid., §27.

[23]Ibid., §§57, 61.

[24]Ibid., §§59, 60, 63.

[25]John Locke, *An Essay concerning Human Understanding,* Peter H. Niddhitch, ed. (Oxford: Clarendon Press, 1973), 2.27.9.

[26]John W. Yolton, *Locke and the Compass of Human Understanding* (Cambridge: Cambridge University Press, 1970), p. 148.

[27]Locke, *Essay concerning Human Understanding,* 2.27.26.

[28]Ibid., 2.27.26; 2.27.13; see also Yolton, *Locke and the Compass of Human Understanding,* p. 152.

[29]Neither Grotius nor Pufendorf gave a definition of *suum*. Instead, they enumerated a long list of goods that they regarded as belonging to an individual by nature (such as life, body, limbs, liberty, reputation, honor), or, in the case of material objects, as being included in this sphere by the individual's will in accordance with the provisions of civil law in civil society. Grotius, *De Iure Belli ac Pacis,* 1.2.1.5 and 2.17.2.1. Pufendorf gives a similar account, though his catalogue differs slightly from Grotius. See Pufendorf, *De Iure Naturae et Gentium,* 3.1.1. See also Karl Olivecrona, "The Term 'Property' in Locke's Two Treatises of Government," *Archiv fuer Rechts und Sozialphilosophie* (1975), p. LXI/1.

[30]Locke extends the status of natural law to his entire concept of property, to all

sorts of rights wherever the individual's moral power reaches. If man's life is God's property, man is morally responsible to God for his preservation. Therefore, he must also have a right to all things that make this preservation possible (compare Locke, *Two Treatises of Government*, Second Treatise, §194). Thus, the meaning of the term "property" in Locke does not depend upon the objects to which it refers and, consequently, he does not use the term, as some scholars assume, in both a wide and a narrow sense, sometimes as all goods belonging to an individual, sometimes only as material objects (see C.B. Macpherson, *The Political Theory of Possessive Individualism* [Oxford: Oxford University Press, 1962], p. 220 and Jacob Viner, "'Possessive Individualism' as Original Sin," *Canadian Journal of Economics and Political Science*, vol. 29 [1963]: 554). Rather, Locke treats each right separately, as well as all rights together, as property. He is consistent, therefore, when he defines property in the *Essay Concerning Human Understanding* as "a right to any thing" (*Essay concerning Human Understanding*, 4.3.18) and when he assures us in the *Two Treatises* that "By Property I must be understood here, as in other places, to mean that Property which Men have in their Persons as well as Goods" (Locke, *Two Treatises of Government*, Second Treatise, §27; compare Laslett, "Introduction" in Locke, *Two Treatises of Government*, pp. 102-103).

This consistency was well understood by Locke's contemporaries: "Mr Locke means by the word 'property' not only the right which one has to his goods and possessions, but even with respect to his actions, liberty, his life, his body; and, in a word, all sorts of right," Jean Barbeyrac, "An historical and critical account of the science of morality," in *The Law of Nature and Nations, by Samuel Pufendorf,* Jean Barbeyrac, ed., translated by Basil Kennet (London, 1729), p. 4. What makes Barbeyrac's opinion unchallengeable is the fact that this usage of the term "property" was not original to Locke in seventeenth century England. A similar meaning of "property" is to be found in such different authors as Hobbes and Richard Baxter, a radical Puritan theologian (see Thomas Hobbes, *Leviathan*, C.B. Macpherson, ed. [Harmondsworth: Penguin, 1985], ch. 30 and Richard Baxter, *A Holy Commonwealth* [London, 1659], p. 134). On this point, see Laslett's footnote to Locke, *Two Treatises of Government,* Second Treatise, §27 and Viner, "'Possessive Individualism' as Original Sin."

[31] Locke, *Two Treatises of Government,* Second Treatise, §27.
[32] Ibid., §28.
[33] Ibid., §46.
[34] Ibid., §30.
[35] Ibid., §32.
[36] Ibid., §33.
[37] Ibid., §42.
[38] Ibid., §38.
[39] Walter Euchner, *Naturrecht und Politik bei John Locke* (Frankfurt am Mein: Europaesche Verlagsanstalt, 1969), p. 82. See also Karl Olivecrona, "Locke's theory of appropriation," *Philosophical Quarterly,* vol. 24, (1974): 225-26.

[40]Locke, *Two Treatises of Government,* Second Treatise, §56; compare Locke, *Two Treatises of Government,* First Treatise, §54.

[41]See Tully, *Discourse on Property,* p. 120.

[42]This interpretation is in agreement with Locke's theory of making, developed in his *Essay concerning Human Understanding,* 2.26.2; 2.7.10; 3.6.40. See also C.E. Vaughn, *Studies in the History of Political Philosophy before and after Rousseau* (Manchester: Manchester University Press, 1925), vol. 1, p. 174, and Tully, *Discourse on Property,* p. 117.

[43]Locke, *Two Treatises of Government,* Second Treatise, §31.

[44]Ibid., §31.

[45]Ibid., §38.

[46]Ibid., §37.

[47]Ibid., §37, 38.

[48]Ibid., §27.

[49]Pufendorf, *De Jure Naturae et Gentium,* 4.4.11. See also Tully, *Discourse on Property,* pp. 125-26.

[50]Robert Filmer, "Observations upon Hugo Grotius De Jure Belli et Pacis," in Robert Filmer, *Patriarcha and Other Political Works of Sir Robert Filmer,* Peter Laslett, ed. (Oxford: Basil Blackwell, 1949), p. 273.

[51]Locke, *Two Treatises of Government,* Second Treatise, §28.

[52]Ibid., §33.

[53]Ibid., §28, 29.

[54]Ibid., §28.

[55]Ibid., §29.

[56]Ibid., §39.

[57]Ibid., §79.

[58]Ibid., §83.

[59]Filmer, "Patriarcha," p. 63.

[60]Locke, *Two Treatises of Government,* Second Treatise, §29.

[61]Locke, *Two Treatises of Government,* First Treatise, §88.

[62]Ibid., §90.

[63]See Martin Seliger, *Liberal Politics of John Locke* (New York: Praeger, 1968), pp. 174-76.

[64]Locke, *Two Treatises of Government,* First Treatise, §42.

[65]Locke clearly follows Aquinas, *Summa Theologica,* II.II.66.7. See John Dunn, "Justice and the Interpretation of Locke's Political Theory," *Political Studies,* XVI, (1968): 68-87, especially 81.

[66]For Locke's beliefs concerning charity see the testimony left by Lady Masham, printed in Maurice Cranston, *John Locke, A Biography* (New York: MacMillan, 1957), p. 426.

[67]See Locke's "Scheme for a Poor Law," submitted to the Board of Trade in 1697 and subsequently rejected by the Board, in H.R. Fox Bourne, ed., *The Life of John Locke,* vol. II (London: Henry S. King & Co., 1876), pp. 377-91, especially

p. 382.

[68] Locke, *Two Treatises of Government*, First Treatise, §156.

[69] Locke, *Two Treatises of Government*, Second Treatise, §14. Another example of a conventional obligation which can be made in the state of nature and in civil society is that of marriage (see §83).

[70] Ibid., §§85-86. Compare §2, and Locke, *Two Treatises of Government*, First Treatise, §135.

[71] Ibid., §85.

[72] Second Treatise, §28.

[73] Macpherson, *Political Theory of Possessive Individualism*, pp. 215. For a similar interpretation, see also Jeremy Waldron, "'The Turfs my servant has cut'," *The Locke Newsletter*, vol. 13 (1982): 9-20, and Neal Wood, *John Locke and Agrarian Capitalism* (Berkeley: University of California Press, 1984), pp. 85-92.

[74] Macpherson, *Political Theory of Possessive Individualism*, p. 214.

[75] Laslett, "Introduction" in Locke, *Two Treatises of Government*, p. 103.

[76] Locke, *Two Treatises of Government*, Second Treatise, §85.

[77] Peter Laslett, *The World We Have Lost* (London: Methuen, 1965), especially pp. 189-190.

[78] Peter Laslett, "Market Society and Political Theory," *Historical Journal*, VII (1962): 153 and Tully, *Discourse on Property*, p. 14.

[79] Henry Braverman, *Labour and Monopoly Capital; The Degradation of Work in the Twentieth Century* (New York: Monthly Review Press, 1974), p. 70, see also p. 54.

[80] Locke, *Two Treatises of Government*, Second Treatise, §43. See Tully, *Discourse on Property*, pp. 140-41.

[81] Laslett indicates that the position of day laborers visiting the farm to work was the same as that of its permanent members and servants. In other words "a day labourer was made a member of the working family for that day." Laslett, *The World We Have Lost*, p. 15. See also Peter Laslett, *Family Life and Illicit Love in Earlier Generations, Essays in Historical Sociology* (Cambridge: Cambridge University Press, 1977), pp. 72-73.

[82] Keith Tribe, *Land, Labour and Economic Discourse* (London: Routledge & Kegan Paul, 1978), pp. 49-51.

[83] Locke, *Two Treatises of Government*, Second Treatise, §§43, 44.

[84] Locke, *Two Treatises of Government*, First Treatise, §41.

[85] Most scholars assume that these uses of money were found in the state of nature proper (for example, see Laslett, "Introduction" in Locke, *Two Treatises of Government*, p. 101; Macpherson, *Political Theory of Possessive Individualism*, pp. 203-20; and Tully, *Discourse on Property*, pp. 146-54). Although there is no doubt that Locke needed the idea of money in the state of nature proper to explain its use according to the provisions of the law of nature, as a historical phenomenon it belongs to the descriptive part of his doctrine (compare Dunn, *Political Thought of John Locke*, p. 118), where there is no room for the governmentless state of

nature proper. It is thus appropriate to keep in mind that money was introduced under the political power of primitive civil society (see ch. 2, footnote 34 above).

[86] Locke, *Two Treatises of Government*, Second Treatise, §46.

[87] Ibid., §37.

[88] Ibid., §49.

[89] Apart from §50 of the Second Treatise, Locke does not speak of the equality of possessions but rather of the equal right of all people to them (§§29, 30). According to Locke, before the introduction of money people's possessions were not equal because "different degrees of industry were apt to give men possessions in different proportions" (§48). See Seliger, *Liberal Politics of John Locke*, pp. 153-55.

[90] Locke, *Two Treatises of Government*, Second Treatise, §37.

[91] Ibid., §§40, 42, 43.

[92] Ibid., §§36, 40, 41, 48.

[93] Ibid., §37.

[94] Ibid., §§37, 46, 47.

[95] Compare John Locke, "Some Thoughts concerning Reading and Study for a Gentleman," in John Locke, *The Educational Writings of John Locke*, James L. Axtell, ed. (Cambridge: Cambridge University Press, 1968), p. 123, and Locke, *Essay concerning Human Understanding*, 2. 21. 45.

[96] . Locke, *Two Treatises of Government*, Second Treatise, §34. Compare Tully, *Discourse on Property*, p. 150.

[97] For example, see Macpherson, *Political Theory of Possessive Individualism*, p. 235.

[98] Locke, *Two Treatises of Government*, Second Treatise, §111.

[99] Dunn, *Political Thought of John Locke*, p. 248.

[100] Seliger, *Liberal Politics of John Locke*, p. 158.

[101] Locke, *Two Treatises of Government*, Second Treatise, §26.

[102] Compare Tully, *Discourse on Property*, pp. 151-153.

[103] Locke, *Two Treatises of Government*, Second Treatise, §135.

[104] Ibid., §135.

[105] Ibid., §135.

[106] Ibid., §6.

[107] Ibid., §171. Compare §§123, 131, 239.

[108] Ibid., §120.

[109] Ibid., §129.

[110] Ibid., §130.

[111] Ibid., §150.

[112] Ibid., §120.

[113] Ibid., §136. Compare §138.

[114] Ibid., §3

[115] See Melvin Cherno, "Locke on Property," *Ethics*, 68, pp. 51-5; Olivecrona, "Locke's Theory of Appropriation," pp. 220-234; and Tully, *Discourse on*

Property, p. 165.

[116]For example, see Ellen Frankel Paul, "On the Theory of the Social Contract within the Natural Rights Tradition," *The Personalist* 59 (1978): 9-21 and Eric Mack, "Distributive Justice and the Tensions of Lockeanism," *Social Philosophy and Policy,* vol. 1, Issue 1, (1983): 132-150.

[117]For the best criticism of the distributive justice interpretation of Locke's conventional order, see Alan Ryan, *Property and Political Theory,* (Oxford: Basil Blackwell, 1984), ch. I; Bruno Rea, "John Locke: Between Charity and Welfare Rights," *Journal of Social Philosophy,* XVIII, (1987): 13-26; Govert den Hartogh, "Tully's Locke," *Political Theory,* vol. 18, (1990): 656-672.

[118]Locke, *Two Treatises of Government,* Second Treatise, §173.

[119]Macpherson, *Political Theory of Possessive Individualism,* p. 221.

[120]Locke's discussion of property is considered within the framework of his polemic with Filmer by Laslett, "Introduction" in Locke, *Two Treatises of Government,* pp. 92-94, 100 and Dunn, *Political Thought of John Locke,* pp. 88-94. The author who stresses that Locke's main purpose in discussing the issue was to reject the Filmerian unity of power and property is Richard Ashcraft, *Locke's Two Treatises of Government* (London: Allen & Unwin, 1987), pp. 81-96. Compare also Ruth W. Grant, *John Locke's Liberalism* (Chicago and London: The University of Chicago Press, 1987), pp. 58-9.

[121]See Tully, *Discourse on Property.*

[122]See footnote 15 above.

[123]See Macpherson, *Political Theory of Possessive Individualism* and Wood, *John Locke and Agrarian Capitalism.*

Chapter 4

The Principles of Civil Society

We have moved from a discussion of the foundations of Filmer's and Locke's systems, where their first and basic elements reside (that is, paternal power or superhuman agency [H^1] and individual or human agency [C^1]), through the presentation of these agencies' standards of rationality, to the application of those standards to the particular issue of property. We can now proceed to consider the second element of their models—the relations prevailing among individuals (H^2 and C^2). Filmer claims these relations are created and defined by paternal power and reflect its standards of rationality; Locke's response is that they are created and defined by individual agents and that they reflect the standards of rationality of these agents.

In further exploring this issue, in this chapter I shall analyze and compare the position of the individual in the political structure according to the doctrines of Filmer and Locke. I shall argue that in Filmer's model the natural status of the individual is that of subjection to paternal power. In Locke's model, the individual is presented as a member of civil society, which results from a conventional arrangement.

I begin with a discussion of the terrestrial sources of political power in the system of each thinker. In Filmer, political power (as any other sort of power) is derived from the superhuman agency—paternal power. Locke rejects this position, casting human agency—the individual—as the only source of political power. He traces the political power of civil society back to the two natural powers that individuals exercise in the state of nature: the power to preserve himself and others, and to punish transgressors of the law of nature. Having thus set the stage, I continue with an analysis of the extent of political power. In Filmer this power is unlimited, but in Locke it is restricted, since individuals specify its extent in the act of social contract. In elaborating on the limited character of political power, Locke rejects Filmer's stand on law and freedom and presents an outline of his own. In that context, he discusses the issue of royal prerogative. I then discuss the question of political obligation and political legitimacy. In Filmer, both have an unconditional character, since they are based upon the existence of natural political duty and natural political authority. Against Filmer, Locke maintains that political obligation and political legitimacy are conditional, since they result from the presence of natural political duties and the absence of any natural political authority. In pursuing this point, Locke points to the consent of individuals as the foundation of both political obligation and political legitimacy. He proceeds to defend—against Filmer's criticism—the notions of express and tacit consent as well as majority rule. Finally, I present the character of the political structure in Filmer and Locke. The adherence of the individual to the Filmerian polity is compulsory, while Locke emphasizes the voluntary association of individuals in civil society. Locke elaborates on this point by discussing the ways in which individuals may freely enter or leave civil society.

Filmer's point of departure in analyzing the human condition is his fundamental assumption that the natural status of man is one of subjection to paternal power. Accordingly:

> Every man that is born, is so far from being free-born, that by his very birth he becomes a subject to him that begets him: under which subjection he is always to live, unless by immediate appointment from God, or by the grant or death of his Father, he become possessed of that power to which he was subject.[1]

However, if an individual becomes a father and exercises paternal power over his children, this does not mean that his natural status has changed; he is still a subject of his ruler, who embodies "the supreme fatherhood." This subjection is independent of the particular form or structure of government and even of the presence of government itself. It is an immanent component of the human condition, for, as Filmer claims:

The Principles of Civil Society

It is a truth undeniable, that there cannot be any multitude of men whatsoever, either great, or small, though gathered together from the several corners and remotest regions of the world, but that in the same multitude, considered by itself, there is one man amongst them that in nature hath a right to be the King of all the rest... and all the others subject unto him.[2]

In defining man's natural status as subjection, Filmer attains a crucial theoretical achievement in his holistic model. Despite his orthodox preference for absolute monarchy, he extends the sanction of God-given natural order to all existing political structures. By doing so, he succeeds in rendering the questions of political legitimacy and political obligation closed to intellectual speculation, since, in presenting man's attachment to any political structure as unconditional, he makes political legitimacy and political obligation unconditional.

Locke's response to these claims is straightforward, though conventional. It is based upon the ontological cliché commonly accepted within the Thomist tradition and among seventeenth century natural law theorists: man lives his life in two different orders: that of nature and that of convention. Accordingly, political legitimacy and political obligation must be conditional, for they depend upon the relations between these two orders.

The Lockean man belongs to the God-given natural order. As God's workmanship and property, he owes his moral status to his Maker. The provisions of the law of nature indicate how he should preserve this status by fulfilling his duties toward God and by executing his rights in relation to his fellow men.

At the same time, the Lockean man belongs to another order, a conventional one that he creates himself. In this conventional order, God plays no part; there is only man enjoying his God-given moral status. Man creates this order for his own purposes, just as God created the natural order for his divine end. We do not know God's purpose in creating the universe, but we do know that man makes his political structure—civil society—in order to set up institutional guarantees that enable him to lead his life according to the law of nature.[3]

For Locke, civil society is a body of individuals united in the act of social contract that has at its disposal political power and is led by its majority. Civil society is that which establishes civil government (which is a set of institutions, including the legislative, executive, federative, and royal prerogative) and is thus to be distinguished from it.

That man creates civil society for his own end indicates that he is its highest value. It is he who is the bridge between the norms of the natural order and the structure of the conventional one; this solution makes possible the extension of moral philosophy into politics.[4] Locke lays down a set of principles upon which civil society should rest if, as the basis of all acceptable forms of government, it is to be in a position to carry out the end for which it is set up—that is, to promote life according to the law of nature. Each of these principles is, in itself, aimed against the rules governing Filmer's concept of man as a subject of paternal power. These principles state that: (1) the individual is the only source of political power; (2) political power is limited; (3) the consent of individuals is the only criterion of the legitimacy of the political power exercised over them; and (4) their adherence to the political structure is voluntary.

The individual as the only source of political power

Throughout his writings, Filmer continually presses upon his reader the claim that "all power on earth is either derived or usurped from the fatherly power, there being no other original to be found of any power whatsoever."[5] The aim of his persistence is fairly clear. Without the supposition that power is to be found outside human beings, Filmer's claim that subjection is not only the natural but also the sole status of man could not hold. Only with this supposition can man be forever locked in subjection; any admission of the alternative supposition, that power originates in man, would destroy Filmer's claim about the exclusiveness of man's natural status and thereby undermine his entire holistic model of social relations. Indeed, if man could be a source of power, then despite having been born to subjection, he could use this power to grant himself another, more favorable status—a status outside the natural order, in a conventional structure created by himself according to his own purpose and will. Under such conditions, political legitimacy and political obligation could not retain their unconditional character.

Locke was well aware of how crucial this position on the source of power was to the structure of his adversary's holistic model. From Filmer's model, based on paternal power, came the claim that, as Locke put it, "we are all born Slaves, and we must continue to be so; there is no remedy for it."[6] To refute this claim, Locke begins by identifying the individual as "another Original of Political Power," thereby indicating "another rise of Government," an alternative to paternal power as the source of government's legitimacy.[7]

Locke claims that in the state of nature there cannot be any subordination among men. "In respect of Jurisdiction or Domination" nobody can be "subjected to the Will or Authority of any other Man."[8] If, as Locke admits, everybody is "equal to the greatest," it is safe to assume that individuals in the state of nature enjoy all the attributes of sovereigns.[9] Each man embodies the complete personal unity of right, might, and decision making. Under the provisions of natural law, he enjoys his individual natural rights by exercising his individual natural powers. He is also entitled by nature to make his own individual decisions on how best to do this.

The Lockean man has natural rights to life, liberty, and the goods necessary to preserve himself,[10] which are, as has been shown, protected by his two natural powers: "the first is to do whatsoever he thinks fit for the preservation of himself and others within the permission of the *Law of Nature*," and the second is "*to punish the Crimes* committed against that Law."[11] Locke's discussion of the two natural powers is the peak of his methodological individualism; its implications are such that he himself admits that his achievement may "seem a very strange Doctrine."[12] Yet a careful analysis of these powers shows that this individualism implies their public as well as private status. In their form they are private, but in their content and extent they are public. That individuals defend their individual rights by exercising their individual powers is not meant to suggest that each individual protects only his own rights, or that he, defending them, uses only his own powers; rather, these powers serve to execute the natural law that binds the whole of mankind. Individuals are bound to protect their own natural rights, but this is only due to Locke's distribution of the basic imperative of the law of nature, the preservation of mankind.[13] Thus, the use of their natural powers, though privately exercised, has not a private but a public dimension.

This is especially evident when Locke discusses the second natural power. There are two reasons to punish offenders against the law of nature: reparation and restraint.[14] In the case of reparation, punishment should be treated as a means toward a private end, namely the compensation due to the injured party, to which this party is entitled by his natural individual right of self-preservation. But in the case of restraint, the end of punishment is public and originates in the natural right to preserve all mankind.[15] The punishment takes place in order to punish the crime, that is, to make the offender suffer for the crime because he deserves it,[16] and to "prevent its being committed again."[17] Locke emphasizes the public content and extent of the second natural power when he includes in it the power to kill another whenever the "heinousness" of his crime "requires" and "deserves" it.[18] Exercising this power should "deter others from doing the like Injury... by the Example of the punishment that attends it from every body, and so *to secure* Men from the attempts of a Criminal."[19]

Thus, while the state of nature lacks the benefits of political power, remedy against its inconveniences emerges from the two natural powers residing within each of its individual members. When individuals in the state of nature unify under the social contract which forms civil society, they transfer their individual powers to that society, thus creating its political power. From the first natural power to enjoy "all the Rights... of the Law of Nature"[20] and "to do whatsoever [an individual] thinks fit for the preservation of himself and others,"[21] arises the first two main requisites of political power in civil society: (1) rule by established, standing laws promulgated to the people, and (2) indifferent and upright judges who decide controversies by reference to these laws. The second natural power "to judge of, and punish the breaches of that Law in others"[22] (which in the state of nature was exercised individually, with each person as a "Judge for himself and Executioner"[23]) becomes the third requisite of political power: (3) employment of the force of the community in the execution of these laws at home, and in the prevention of injuries and other encroachments on members' rights in foreign affairs.[24]

Thus, the *conditio sine qua non* of the establishment of civil society is a redistribution of the sovereign attributes which belong to every individual in the state of nature. This redistribution means that the unity of right, might, and decision-making within each individual ends. Individual natural rights become individual civil rights supported by the authority of civil society.[25] The might of individuals is subsumed by collective political power, without which civil society could not exist.[26] Decision-making becomes the exclusive right of the majority, and the duration of civil society is conditional upon their activity.[27] Due to this redistribution, civil society has now "in itself the Power to preserve the Property, and in order thereunto to punish the Offenses of all those of that Society."[28]

The only way by which civil society can replace the state of nature is the act of social contract, through which "any one divests himself of his Natural Liberty, and *puts on the bonds of Civil Society*... by agreeing with other Men to joyn and unite into a Community."[29] This is possible only when each man gives up his two natural powers to civil society.[30]

This transfer creates political power. The content of this power is the same as that of the two natural powers given up by individuals, but its status differs from theirs. The two natural powers of individuals are public because of their content and extent, but they are private in their terrestrial roots. Political power, on the other hand, owes its status to the fact that it is public in its content, its extent, and its roots. As Locke points out, "*this power has its Original only from the Compact* and Agreement, and the mutual Consent of those who make up the Community."[31] Thus, the origin of political power is to be found only in the acts of individuals entering a social contract. Indeed, political power is a part of the individual's natural sphere which he hands over by his decision. Locke, not wanting to leave any doubt about this, writes that "*Political Power* is that Power which every Man, having in the state of Nature, has given up into the hands of Society."[32]

The claim that the individual is the source of political power is a matter of fundamental significance for Locke's concept of civil society. He returns to this issue many times because, as he puts it, "in this we have the original *right and rise* of both *the Legislative and Executive Power,* as well as of the Governments and Societies themselves":[33] civil society is based upon the natural rights of individuals. The same power that takes its normative status and moral character from the defense of individual natural rights in the state of nature preserves the same rights in civil society, though in a different form for reasons of better efficiency.

Political power is limited

From the discussion thus far, it is clear that on Filmer's view the only authority human beings are under is paternal power. Provided that paternal power is also the only distributor of might and right, which do not originate anywhere else, it can be concluded that this power must be unlimited. Indeed, there is no other right or might that could contain it.

Filmer himself reaches the same conclusion in a slightly different manner, referring in this context to paternal power not as the only authority but as the supreme one. He writes:

> As the scripture teacheth us, that the supreme power was originally in the Fatherhood without any limitation, so likewise reason doth evidence it, that if God ordained that supremacy should be, that then supremacy must of necessity be unlimited: for the power that limits must be above that power which is limited; if it be limited, it cannot be supreme: so that if [one] will grant supreme power to be the ordinance of God, the supreme power will prove itself to be unlimited by the same ordinance, because a supreme limited power is a contradiction.[34]

In arguing for limited government, Locke bases his rejection of Filmer's position on two claims. The first states that political power in civil society is confined to the sphere given up by individuals in the act of social contract. It is the individuals, then, and not civil society or the holders of political power themselves who specify its extent. The second claim indicates that the natural rights of individuals are defended by the authority of civil society and specified by the provisions of positive law, but the rights themselves remain within the individuals.

In Locke, an individual incorporating himself into civil society gives up, to differing extents, both of his natural powers. The second power, that of punishing the crimes committed against the natural law, he gives up wholly.[35] The first, that "of doing whatever he thought fit for the Preservation of himself, and the rest of Mankind," he gives up only "so far forth as the preservation of himself, and the rest of that Society shall require."[36] The result of this distinction is the arrangement according to which the individual's natural powers are divided. One part is transformed into political power that is at civil society's disposal. The other part remains at the disposal of civil society's individual members. Locke chooses this option because he wants to leave a part of individual's natural powers on the side of individual natural rights. In civil society, these rights are conventionally specified but remain beyond the extent of civil society's political power because they are not the object of social contract.

The justification of Locke's solution may be considered in two stages. The first concerns only the power of judging how rights are preserved in civil society. An individual does not subordinate his rights to civil society, because the proper enjoyment of them is the condition for his fulfilling his duties toward God. The individual's rights are guarded and protected by civil society, but this fact does not free the Lockean man from his responsibility to his Maker for the preservation of himself and his fellow human beings. The fulfillment of the duty of preservation requires constant vigilance on the part of the members of civil society. The power to preserve mankind is the necessary means that enables them to carry out this task. "God and Nature" never allow "a man so to abandon himself as to neglect his own preservation." Thus, "the Body of the People, or any single Man... have, by a Law antecedent and paramount to all positive Laws of men, reserv'd... to themselves... to judge" whether their rights are jeopardized.[37]

The second stage of the model for limited political power goes further and deals with the central issue, namely, why natural rights themselves are inalienable. The solution to this problem is based upon the absolute and categorical prohibition of suicide[38] that lies at the heart of the normative part of Locke's doctrine. Men are the "property" of their Maker; only he (and not they) should determine when they should die. Thus, man is "bound to preserve himself"; neither he nor other humans can alienate his rights. Accordingly, in the state of nature he possesses "an uncontrollable Liberty to dispose of his Person or Possessions, yet he has not Liberty to destroy himself."[39] In the state of nature the prohibition of suicide already has a wide public dimension: man has neither a natural right nor a natural power to take his own life since human life is God's property, and only he has that right and that power. Locke states that "he that cannot take away his own Life, cannot give another power over it," that is, he cannot consent to his own slavery by putting himself "under the Absolute, Arbitrary Power of another."[40]

While the prohibition of suicide is the basis of the model for limited government, it does not explain—at least in terms of the normative principles of Locke's doctrine—how and why civil society can perform its main task, that of the preservation of its members. Indeed, if Locke had finished his discussion of the making of civil society at this point, his polity could hardly have enjoyed the attributes of a sovereign state, to which the power of punishing offenders, including the power of imposing the death penalty, was ascribed by every seventeenth century political thinker. This was the issue Filmer used to argue for the apparently inevitable contradiction between the normative foundation of civil society expressed by the suicide taboo and the coercive character of political power. As Filmer, a penetrating critic of the contractarian model, put it:

> If no man have power to take away his own life without the guilt of being a murderer of himself, how can any people confer such a power as they have not themselves upon any one man, without being accessories to their own deaths, and every particular man become guilty *felo de se*?[41]

To understand how Locke, using the contractarian framework, tries to combine the principle of limited political power over innocent members of civil society with the authority of that society to impose the death penalty on transgressors of the law, I will consider the power given up by individuals entering civil society in two cases. In the first, the power to destroy the innocent cannot be turned over to civil society either by that individual or by his fellow members. In the second, the power to put a transgressor to death cannot be derived from the transgressor himself either. Regardless of the number of acts deserving death that he may have committed, the transgressor still has no "power to part with... this Fundamental, Sacred, and unalterable Law of *Self-Preservation*."[42] The rule that the transgressor cannot punish himself also originates in the suicide taboo. Although there is no doubt that the transgressor does not belong to mankind as understood by Locke—that is, to a peaceful, moral community of people "capable of the Law of Nature"[43]—the precise time when he loses his human, normative status is not clearly specified. He has been treated as a "beast" by his fellow human beings since he committed the offense, but it is only when he is captured by the innocent that he is freed from his natural duty of self-preservation. The transgressor can thus only be punished by the power given up by the innocent entering civil society. This solution, which appears to follow from Locke's premises, does not provide a satisfactory answer to Filmer's question. It is reached using the framework of civil society as set up in the act of social contract, but it is not formulated within this framework. In other words, the act of social contract, which constitutes the transfer of the two individual natural powers and the creation of political power, is completely irrelevant to this solution. The transgressor is punished by the joint power of civil society, regardless of whether he is a party to the social contract or not, or of whether he is a subject of this commonwealth or is an alien who commits an offense against it.[44]

Despite his frequent use of the extreme example of the offender deserving of death, which is part of the radical rhetoric accompanying his final model for the right to resist and to punish the absolute monarch, Locke also sees another aspect of the right of civil society to punish offenses. He is well aware that the necessity of punishing smaller crimes, the commission of which do not cause the complete loss of the criminal's rights, may lead to an abuse of political power and to a violation of these rights that can go beyond the end of proper punishment.[45] At this point, Locke again states his model for limited political power by referring to the act of social contract. Since in the state of nature no man has the "Absolute or Arbitrary Power, to use a Criminal when he has got him in his hands, according to the passionate heats, or boundless extravagancy of his own Will"[46] and since "no body can give more Power than he has himself,"[47] civil society's ability to punish is restricted by the extent of its power and by the way in which this power can be exercised. As in the state of nature, so in civil society; the offender ought to be punished as the holder of political power "soberly judges the Case to require."[48] This judgment should be passed "so far as calm reason and conscience dictates."[49]

Having stated in the act of social contract the structural barrier against the appearance of arbitrary rule in civil society, Locke goes on to place another obstacle in its way—the legal barrier. In this context, his account of law in civil society offers a rejection of the notion of law in Filmer's polity. Filmer treats law exclusively as a means of paternal power. In arguing against the limited power of the king, Filmer writes:

to govern, is to give the law to others, and not to have a law given to govern and limit him that governs.[50]

Contrary to those

who believe that the first invention of laws was to bridle and moderate the over-great power of Kings... the truth is [that] the original of laws was for the keeping of the multitude in order.[51]

In challenging this understanding of law, Locke describes both the natural law in the state of nature and the positive law in civil society as the "fence" that prevents man from being "subject to the inconstant, uncertain, unknown, Arbitrary Will of another man."[52] In each case, the provisions of law draw a clear distinction between behavior in accord with them, and behavior that follows unhindered capricious desires. The former serves the preservation of mankind because it takes place within the sphere of duties and rights. The latter is placed beyond this sphere; it rises from a normative vacuum. Arbitrary rule falls into the category of impermissible behavior and hence is incompatible with the rule of law.

This distinction expresses Locke's twofold account of law. If law is regarded from the standpoint of an individual who does not intend to follow its provisions, its character must be negative. It forbids his acts in order to preserve others against his violence.[53] On the other hand, as Locke stresses, an agent who wants to enjoy the benefits of the law must find its character profoundly positive.[54] For him, "Law, in its true Notion, is not so much the Limitation as *the direction of a free and intelligent Agent* to his proper Interest, and prescribes no farther than is for the general Good."[55] He governs himself by its provisions, within which his reason makes him aware "how far he is left to the freedom of his will."[56] Indeed, the law protects him only from "Bogs and Precipices"; such protection should not be thought of as confinement since, according to the law's provisions, he has "a *Liberty* to dispose, and order, as he lists, his Person, Actions, Possessions, and his whole Property."[57]

Locke believes that the presence of law is a necessary condition of the existence of freedom. He states this belief (which applies to the state of nature as well as to civil society), clearly rejecting Filmer's suggestion that freedom is "*A Liberty for every one to do what he lists, to live as he pleases, and not to be tyed by any Laws.*"[58] Locke calls this not freedom but license—a state which lacks any constraints;[59] in his view, freedom extends only to men who are subjects of law.

Like his account of law, the notion of freedom that Locke formulates has two aspects.[60] The first, the negative aspect, is expressed as freedom from interference by others. In the state of nature, man enjoys liberty so understood when he is "free from any superior Power of Earth" and is not "under the Will of Legislative Authority of Man" but has "only the Law of Nature for his Rule." Under these conditions, the only threat to negative individual liberty comes from fellow individuals toward whom the law of nature cannot be properly executed. As soon as civil society is established, the threat to an individual's negative freedom comes not so much from fellow members of civil society as from civil government.[61] Accordingly, "The *Liberty of Man, in Society*, is to be under no other Legislative Power, but that established, by consent, in the Common-wealth, nor under the Domination of any Will, or Restraint of any Law, but what the Legislative shall enact."[62] The concept of negative freedom has a very public, political character and, as such, is included in the structural barrier that in Locke's view, is set up in the act of social contract and protects the members of civil society from arbitrary rule. This "Freedom from Absolute, Arbitrary Power" which "is so necessary to, and closely joyned with a Man's Preservation"[63] can be established only under the rule of law, which is possible only in civil society. In other words, negative freedom can be achieved only by the collective effort of individuals expressed in the act of social contract; an individual cannot accomplish it by himself.

The second aspect of freedom, the positive, rests upon the idea of self-determination and is described by Locke as "a Liberty to follow my own Will in all things, where the Rule prescribes not."[64] As such, it is logically dependent upon the existence of negative freedom; nobody can act according to his own will if he is under absolute, arbitrary rule. In this sense, an individual's positive freedom depends upon the conditions created by him in cooperation with others. In civil society the rule of law maximizes both aspects of liberty because *"the end of Law* is not to abolish or restrain, but *to preserve and enlarge Freedom."*[65] Yet positive freedom, unlike negative, cannot be guaranteed to the Lockean man by any provision of law. Rather, it must be achieved by his individual efforts, since it results from the principles of workmanship, the principles of man's individual responsibility toward God.[66]

Locke's concepts of law and liberty interact and finally come together in civil society. The two concepts together outline the boundaries between the extent of political power and the rights of members of civil society; political power should "be exercised by *established and promulgated Laws*: that both the People may know their Duty, and be safe and secure within the Limits of the Law, and the Rulers too kept within their due bounds."[67] But because political power emerges from the very construction of Locke's social contract and is thus prior to positive law, positive law does not set up political power, it only makes it more precise.

This is not without consequences for Locke, who then interjects the concept of the royal prerogative into his system. Locke's royal prerogative appears to mitigate his stand against arbitrary power, which he defines as that which is exercised "without *declared* and *received Laws*."[68] He claims that arbitrary power cannot be completely removed from civil society because its remedy, the rule of law, can perform its function only to a limited extent, for it is circumscribed by its own imperfection. The defects of the positive law are such that rigorously following its provisions may, at times, contradict the principles of the law of nature and the ends of civil society. Thus, the main shortcomings of municipal laws—their generality, silence, and rigidity—can be compensated for by the royal prerogative,[69] which is, as Locke admits, "an Arbitrary Power... left in the Prince's hand."[70]

This qualification, however, requires explanation. If the status of the royal prerogative is seen through the lens of positive law, it must be judged to be an arbitrary power. Indeed, its exercise, which is a response to unpredictable social and political necessities, is based upon the private judgment of the monarch. As such, not only does it take place outside the system of positive law, it is sometimes even aimed "against the direct letter of that Law."[71] Yet the prerogative cannot be taken for an arbitrary power if judged from the perspective of the natural law, a perspective that Locke treats as sufficiently "declared and received." The right of prerogative is simply the monarch's power to directly execute the law of nature.[72] Thus, like the natural power of individuals in the state of nature, it must be exercised in accordance with the law of nature, and its extent is, limited by the imperative of the "Fundamental Law of Nature and Government," according to which "as much as may be, All the Members of the Society are to be *preserved*."[73]

Nevertheless, the royal prerogative marks an exception to the whole contractarian model of the *Two Treatises:* it is the only sort of political power that may go beyond the prescribed border in safeguarding the inalienable rights of the members of civil society. Thus, its arbitrary character is sometimes backed up by its truly absolute content: by the right of prerogative, for example, "an innocent Man's House" may be pulled down to "stop the Fire, when the next to it is burning."[74] In such specific cases, where the monarch exercises his power in a way which is arbitrary (against the law of nature) and absolute (violating natural rights), an individual is faced with might which, as Locke describes elsewhere, is placed over his "Person and Estate"—in other words, a might which makes his preservation difficult or even impossible. This is an extreme situation, in which an innocent man who joined civil society to be free from the absolute, arbitrary power of others and to preserve the natural rights granted to him by natural law, is deprived of those rights by an absolute, arbitrary power backed up by the authority of civil society. Yet even when the royal prerogative destroys the means of an individual's preservation, as in the aforementioned case, it still executes the law of nature in the context of civil society. This law allows the rights of individuals to be sacrificed in order to secure the preservation of mankind, which in civil society takes the form of the public good.[75]

Though it is established in civil society for a worthy end, the features of the power of royal prerogative are the same as the attributes of the power of the absolute monarch. Yet in spite of its absolute content and arbitrary character, Locke believes the power of prerogative (unlike that of the absolute monarch) to be well reconciled with civil society. This compatibility can be explained only by the fact that—in spite of its occasional violations of the natural rights of individual members of civil society—the prerogative operates within the proper limits of political power as a whole. As Locke points out, "the Bounds of the *Prerogative*" are "the Bounds of the publick good."[76] What makes this compatibility possible is the very fact that this limitation can be imposed upon the power of prerogative in the political practice of civil society.[77]

Consent of individuals as the only criterion of the legitimacy of political power

Filmer's discussion of political obligation and political legitimacy is very brief and straightforward. It consists of two elements. The first states the duty of man to obey his rulers; this duty is natural, since paternal power is by "a general binding ordinance settled by God" in every ruler.[78] The second deals with political authority, which is also natural; Filmer writes:

> In all kingdoms or commonwealths in the world, whether the Prince be the supreme Father of the people or but the true heir of such a Father, or whether he come to the Crown by usurpation, or by election of the nobles or of the people, or by any other way whatsoever, or whether some few or a multitude govern the commonwealth, yet still the authority that is in any one, or

in many, or in all of these, is the only right and natural authority of a supreme Father.[79]

In sum, both political obligation and political legitimacy are unconditional.[80]

Rejecting the position of his adversary, Locke denies that political duties and political authority are both natural. Rather, he claims, political duties have a natural character, but political authority does not.

In Locke, the natural character of political duties is based on the place of political power in the hierarchy of rights and duties that spans the natural and conventional order. At the top of this hierarchy is God's right to man, as his workmanship and property. This right creates man's correlative duty toward God—the natural duty to preserve himself and the rest of mankind. That duty leads to man's natural right of self-preservation, specified in his rights of life, liberty, and estate, which impose correlative duties on the part of others to respect these individual rights. Political power is a conventional emanation of the individuals' right of self-preservation, because it has been authorized, through the act of social contract, to enforce the duties of others to respect man's natural rights. (Locke makes this point very clear when he calls political power a "right"[81]). Thus, the political duties of an individual, or his duties toward the conventional institution of political power, are generated from his natural duty to preserve mankind, and this duty results from the need to enforce God's right to his workmanship. Before writing the *Two Treatises,* Locke had already claimed that man's political duties result from his duty toward God:

> if he finds that God has made him & all other men in a state wherein they cannot subsist without society and has given them judgment to discern what is capable of preserving that society, can he but conclude that he is obliged and that God requires him to follow those rules which conduce to the preserving of society?[82]

If Locke had assumed, as Filmer did, that there were not only natural political duties but also natural authority, he would surely have finished his discussion of political obligation and political legitimacy at this point. Indeed, he would have indicated that men are naturally obliged to obey those who are naturally entitled to be obeyed, since their power is naturally legitimate. However, Locke's discussion of political obligation and political legitimacy was much richer than that, since he based it upon a different set of premises. He presupposed that natural political duties are not accompanied by any natural political authority, because men are equal in respect to their God-given moral status. This status rules out any natural subordination among them.[83] Thus, men are naturally obliged to obey but there is no terrestrial agent who is naturally entitled to be obeyed, since power cannot be naturally legitimate. This is the reason that despite the admission of the existence of natural political duties, Locke bases political obligation on the individual consent of those who set up or join civil society. Locke thus concludes that, contrary to Filmer's claims, political obligation and political legitimacy are conditional.

In the *Two Treatises,* unlike in his earlier writings,[84] Locke does not discuss the concept of consent as a subject in itself. Rather, he uses the term in a remarkably nonspecific way,[85] applying it to many different states of affairs, when very different sorts of obligations are created. Accordingly, men are said to give their consent to their marriage, to the rise of a money economy, to their property arrangements, to their membership in civil society, and to their representatives when they choose them in that society, and they are also said to express their consent when these representatives make laws, especially tax laws. However, political obligation depends exclusively upon that consent which makes man leave the state of nature and join civil society. Only this consent provides a reason for claiming that a particular individual at a particular time accepts some concrete civil society as legitimate and, thus, as entitled to his obedience.

To digress for a moment, I wish to comment on a strong tendency in scholarship, a tendency to question the central role of consent as the foundation of Locke's construction of political obligation. The claim shared by such scholars as J. P. Plamenatz, J. W. Gough, Hanna Pitkin, and John Dunn,[86] who follow this tendency, is that the real source of political obligation is the character of the government—namely, whether or not it respects the provisions of the law of nature in political practice, thereby promoting the public good and operating within the limits outlined in the act of social contract. If these conditions are met, they claim, then the personal consent given by individuals entering civil society is either essentially irrelevant to the legitimacy of that society (as in the extreme position of Pitkin) or not a source of such legitimacy but only a precondition that makes the behavior of the government licit and acceptable to civil society's members (as in the moderate position taken by Dunn).

The assumption which underlies both of these positions is that the illegitimacy of tyranny is greater than that of usurpation. Accordingly, one should admit that although a tyrant's power can never be legitimate because his rule is against the law of nature, the situation of the usurper is different. The usurper may legitimize his power if he governs according to that law. It is true that neither a tyrant nor a usurper enjoys the consent of the members of civil society; yet the power of the usurper, if he respects the law of nature, is compatible with the ends of civil society. Thus, he can be resisted only under the condition that the consequence of such resistance is likely to benefit rather than harm others.[87]

It would be difficult to find in the premises of Locke's construction of consent a confirmation of the option these scholars ascribe to him. When the Lockean man consents to something, this may mean agreeing, endorsing, acquiescing, willing, or accepting. But when he gives his consent to enter civil society, it can only mean that he agrees to surrender his two natural powers, because "there, and only there is *Political Society* where every one of the Members hath quitted this natural Power, resign'd it up into the hands of the Community."[88] Thus, since the consent to join civil society always implies the transfer of his natural powers, that consent is the sole cause of political obligation toward the concrete civil society and its ruler. In other words, this consent is not simply a precondition for the legitimacy of a particular civil society; it is both the necessary and a sufficient condition for legitimacy. Consent would be a mere precondition if an individual passively subjected himself to a certain power exercised over the civil society which he entered, gave up his political initiative to this power, and waited to see what would happen. However, such individuals are not found in Locke's *Two Treatises*. The Lockean man deliberately transfers his individually exercised public power to civil society, that is, he participates from the very beginning in the exercise of political power. In Locke, nobody can treat his own consent to political power in civil society as his preconditional acceptance of it and, at the same time, participate in its exercise. Accordingly, a lack of participation excludes consent just as a lack of consent rules out participation. If a ruler turns tyrannical, the Lockean man stops participating in the government's power and withdraws his consent. Similarly, his consent ceases and participation comes to an end when a usurper seizes political power in civil society. Thus, both usurper and tyrant exercise a power to which they have no right.[89] Accordingly, each is, in the same way and to the same extent, an illegitimate ruler. Each "is but a single private Person without Power, and without Will, that has any Right to *Obedience*."[90]

Thus, it is unfounded to claim—as do the aforementioned scholars— that it is possible to base political obligation and political legitimacy in Locke's system upon something other than the consent of individuals. His contractarian model leaves no room for such an interpretation. In his model, political power always enjoys both a moral character and a normative status. Thus, if the usurper rules according to the law of nature, while his power can attain the moral character that legitimate political power enjoys, it will still find itself in a normative vacuum. The usurper's power cannot obtain the normative status of political power since it is not a link in the chain of the transfer of power, which leads from God through individuals to civil society. Thus, the interpretation under discussion is not valid unless the scholars who endorse it assume the presence in Locke's system of a kind of natural political authority that is automatically enjoyed by those who rule according to the law of nature. Such an assumption would ascribe to Locke the very position against which he argued in his dispute with Filmer.

This does not mean that Locke ignores the fact that men have historically paid obedience to holders of power to whom they did not give their consent. But this obedience is generated from the fact of their submission, which Locke rigorously distinguishes from consent.[91] Consent is the creation of a right on the part of the ruler; submission is merely an acknowledgment of the fact that the ruler has the physical capacity to exercise his power. This fact, like any other, belongs to the descriptive and not to the normative part of Locke's doctrine, and as such it does not create either a ruler's rights or subjects' duties. Yet nothing prevents this fact from putting into operation norms that have already been established independently of it. Subjects have a duty to obey rulers to whom they did not consent in a situation where resistance is impossible and where a refusal of such obedience could cause a threat to their preservation. However, this obligation is not the political obligation owed by citizens to their chosen political authority. Rather, this is a natural obligation derived directly from the natural duty of self-preservation man owes to God.

Having clarified the issue of the importance of consent in Locke's contractarianism, we can now move on to discuss the details of his response to Filmer. While basing political obligation on the consent of individuals, Locke had to answer Filmer's questions about "the manner of the peoples passing their consent" and consequently about the determination of, as Filmer put it,

> which of them is sufficient, and which not to make a right or title; whether it must be antecedent to possession, or may be consequent: express, or tacite: collective, or representative: absolute, or conditionated: free, or enforced: recoverable, or irrecoverable.

These issues, Filmer argued,

would not have been neglected, considering how necessary it is to resolve the conscience, touching the manner of the peoples passing their consent; and what is sufficient, and what not, to make, or derive a right, or title from the people.[92]

Locke begins his response with the distinction between tacit and express consent. This difference is not just confined to the manner in which the consent is given; rather, Locke connects it to several consequences that fully cover the wide range of problems raised by Filmer. Yet Locke's demonstration of this distinction is unquestionably the most carelessly presented theoretical sequence of the *Two Treatises* and, as such, leaves so many logical inconsistencies, even contradictions, that it is completely impossible for interpreters to build up a clear, precise, and well-structured concept of his answer to Filmer's challenge.

The purpose of Locke's exposition of express consent is to indicate that an individual who gives it manifests his unequivocal intention to associate himself with a particular civil society and to accept all the duties that result from membership in it. "Nobody doubts," writes Locke, that only "an express Consent, of any Man, entering into any Society, makes him a perfect Member of that Society, a Subject of that Government."[93] He makes this point more precise and suggests that express consent guarantees the status of membership because it is the same sort of consent as that given by the founders of civil society.[94] Thus, it should be assumed that he treated this consent not as a hypothetical event but rather as an explicit public manifestation of will, regarded as a sociological fact.[95] This understanding of express consent seems to be in agreement with the interpretation of Paul Russell, who claims that Locke understood such consent to be simply a verbal declaration, as did the two other natural law and social contract theorists, Hobbes and Pufendorf.[96]

However strange it may seem, this is really all that contemporary Locke scholarship is in a position to say about the theoretical aspects of express consent. A seventeenth century English reader could perhaps have found in Locke's presentation a reference to his own political behavior—as, for instance, to the practice of taking an oath of allegiance.[97] He could probably also have extended a theoretical model implied by such references. But this does not change the fact that Locke breaks off his discussion of this subject without any clarification of what distinguishes the status of the member of civil society from that of the rest of the inhabitants of its territory. He gives no instances of the circumstances in which he thinks that express consent may be given, except that of land inheritance.[98] Yet this is itself an extremely unfortunate example. It leaves open the question of the citizenship, not only of the landless population, but also of every landowner who comes by his estate in another way—a lacunae which, given the historical reality of seventeenth century England, must be treated as quite absurd. Moreover, as will be shown below, the example of land inheritance contradicts Locke's discussion of tacit consent.

Contrary to the impression given by Locke that "the difficulty is, what ought to be looked upon as a tacit consent,"[99] his answer to this question is relatively straightforward. Every person who finds himself in a country is held to have tacitly agreed to comply with its laws. Indeed, it can be assumed that Locke shifts all the weight of his discussion of political obligation onto the issue of tacit consent, since the obligation of obedience to the laws applies to members and non-members of civil society alike.

What distinguishes these two groups with respect to political obligation is simply the duration of time for which the laws bind them. Without giving any justification of his position, Locke insists that express consent should be treated as that which binds in perpetuity.[100] In contrast, tacit consent is confined to the period when individuals voluntarily take any advantage of the widely understood benefits of the country. Accordingly:

> Every Man, that hath any Possession, or Enjoyment, of any part of the Dominions of any Government, doth thereby give his *tacit Consent,* and is as far forth obliged to Obedience to the Laws of that Government, during such Enjoyment, as any one under it; whether this his Possession be of Land, to him and his Heirs for ever, or a Lodging only for a Week; or whether it be barely travelling freely on the Highway.[101]

The circumstances in which tacit consent may be given include a wide range of situations and are not by any means limited to or associated with the performance of just one sort of action.[102] The landowner who possesses an estate in the territory of a country is held to acknowledge the jurisdiction of that civil society over his person just as is the traveller who will leave the territory in a couple of days. The character of the political obligation is in both cases temporal, because both are free to decide how long their obedience to that civil society will last. This rule is not changed by the fact that the landowner in his act of tacit consent is also taken to acknowledge the permanent jurisdiction of civil society over his estate. This jurisdiction is not extended over his person.[103]

The aim of Locke's (admittedly poor) presentation of express and tacit consent was to demonstrate that, contrary to Filmer's claims, it was logically valid to claim that the political legitimacy of civil society was based upon the consent of everyone—literally everyone who obeyed the law set up by it (since those who did not obey the positive law placed themselves outside civil society in the same way as those who did not observe the natural law in the state of nature placed themselves outside the community of mankind). Locke's position involves two interacting assumptions, reflected by the introduction of the categories of citizens and non-citizens. The first assumption is the necessity of maintaining the legal status of the founders of civil society, in order to preserve its credibility as an association that was originally created in the political and institutional vacuum of the state of nature. The second assumption is the practical requirement of acknowledging the authority of civil society over all inhabitants of its territory.[104]

Locke's concept of consent—contrary to Filmer's mockery—attempts to illustrate that a rationalistic and individualistic discussion of political power's legitimacy in civil society is logically justifiable. However, since Locke formulates this proof at the level of the individual, he can not solve the whole problem he was approaching. The question that still requires separate consideration is what makes political power in a concrete civil society legitimate. To answer this, Locke has to reconcile three elements of his system: first, the concept of individual consent; second, the notion of collective consent; and third, the requirements of the state's everyday business.

Locke's attempts at clarifying the compatibility of these three elements are a response to Filmer's detailed criticism of the role of consent in social contract theories. Filmer rejected any coexistence of these three elements and indicates that government by consent of the people was not only unstable but logically impossible. The strength of his model lay in his combination of the two axioms of contractarian thought, interpreted literally: the natural equality of men, and the treatment of the people or civil society as the sum of all the individuals who lived in the state's territory. Having combined the two, Filmer could safely challenge the principle of majority rule: "Unless it can be proved by some law of nature that the major, or some other part, have power to overrule the rest of the multitude," he writes, "it must follow that the acts of multitudes not entire are not binding to all, but only to such as consent unto them."[105] Accordingly, he concluded, "it is most unjust to exclude any one man from his right in government; and to suppose the people so unnatural, as at the first to have all consented to give away their right to a major part... is not only improbable, but impossible."[106] The only logical way out of this dilemma would have been the attainment of perfect unanimity.[107] Admitting the need for such absolute unanimity would have ruled out any efforts at decision making because, as Filmer claims, even in the smallest kingdom "all men should spend their whole lives in nothing else but in running up and down to covenant."[108] Having rejected the procedure of majority rule as well as unanimity, Filmer concludes that anarchy is the logical and practical consequence of contractarian arguments. "Not only every city," he stresses, but even "every particular man, [would be at] liberty to choose himself to be his own King if he please; and he were a madman that being by nature free, would choose any man but himself to be his own governor."[109]

Locke's task, then, in discussing the question of the legitimacy of political power in a concrete civil society, was to prove that the principles of natural law could be applied to political practice without doing any damage to the everyday business of the state. This undertaking required him to balance the normative and descriptive parts of his doctrine without sacrificing either the conceptual or the practical aspect of his position. Given the lack of natural political authority, individuals in the act of social contract do not just give up their natural powers to civil society, they also determine a decision-making procedure which is binding on all members of that society and which, thereby, makes the community "one Body, with a Power to Act as one Body."[110] In this way, individual consent (which legitimizes political power at the level of the individual) is transformed into collective consent (which legitimizes it at the level of civil society as a whole). Without this transformation, there would be "still as great a liberty" as an individual "had before his Compact, or any one else in the State of Nature hath, who may submit himself and consent to any acts of it if he thinks fit."[111]

Searching for a suitable decision-making procedure, Locke chooses, not surprisingly, the principle of majority rule as the only acceptable solution.[112] He takes great pains to persuade his reader that the reasons behind his choice are practical, pointing out that the only alternative procedure would be unanimity, which would no doubt make it impossible to preserve civil society at all. "The Infirmities of Health, and Avocations of Business" as well as "the variety of Opinions, and contrariety of Interests" rule out the consent of every individual as a practicable decision-making procedure.[113] Joining a society upon such terms would be "only like *Cato's* coming into the Theatre, only to go out again."[114]

Nevertheless, contrary to this commonsensical (not to say unnecessary) argument in favor of majority rule and against unanimity, Locke alters the strategy of his argument drastically, and claims that the status of the majority is based upon "the Law of Nature and Reason."[115] This ascription of a natural character to majority rule is useless in Locke's

The Principles of Civil Society 89

argument and does not further his exposition. The practical model already outlined is strong enough to indicate that civil society's ability to establish majority rule is a condition of its preservation; the attempt at using the natural law model contains a distinct inconsistency, because the agreement concerning majority rule is part of the act of social contract. As such, it is a conventional institution set up by the will of individuals entering civil society. But the damage Locke does to his system by this statement is much greater than that of merely introducing inconsistency. He undermines the entire contractarian model of the *Two Treatises*. Indeed, when he treats majority rule as a natural institution, he must also acknowledge its "Right to act and conclude the rest,"[116] that is, the right of the majority to impose its decisions upon the minority of civil society as natural. This leads to the approval of a concept of natural political authority, which is precisely what Locke has been arguing against. The reason for this confusion in Locke's presentation of majority rule is clear. He took this step under the pressure of Filmer's criticism—according to which, in a political system based upon the rights of individuals, majority rule could not be legitimate unless it had the status of a natural institution.

The voluntary character of adherence to the political structure

The inevitable consequence of Filmer's concepts of natural political duty and natural political authority, and of his rejection of the idea of consent, is the notion of the polity as a natural structure, adherence to which can never be questioned. Only such a polity is compatible with Filmer's notion of man's natural status of subjection.

Filmer does not feel much need to use any logical model in support of his notion of polity as a compulsory structure and his rejection of the idea of civil society as a voluntary association. In fact, in his critique of contractarian thought, Filmer does not even attack the voluntarist idea, but rather confines himself to indicating that any rejection of his own concepts of natural political duties and natural political authority will inevitably lead to the disintegration of any state. Indeed, Filmer's most efficient weapon in his critique of contractarianism is mockery. He maintains that its first assumption—that it is possible to create a state, and possible for anybody to enter it at any time according to his will—is simply absurd. In illustrating this point, he writes:

> Since nature hath not distinguished the habitable world into kingdoms, nor determined what part of a people shall belong to one kingdom, and what to another, it follows that the original freedom of mankind being supposed, every man is at liberty to be of what kingdom he please, and so every petty company hath a right to make a kingdom by itself.[117]

Filmer then claims that the second assumption of contractarianism—that it is possible for individuals to leave a state that already existed—is equally absurd:

> If it were a thing so voluntary, and at the pleasure of men when they are free to put themselves under subjection, why may they not as voluntarily leave subjection when they please and be free again? If they have liberty to change their natural freedom, into a voluntary subjection, there is stronger reason that they may change their voluntary subjection into natural freedom, since it is lawful for men to alter their wills as their judgments.[118]

In order to avoid any admission of the existence of natural political authority, Locke had to adopt both the assumptions ridiculed by Filmer. Indeed, if civil society is to be treated as a political structure in which man is a free agent, it must be exactly such a voluntary association as Filmer mockingly describes. Locke's position, discussed at length in the *Two Treatises,* is made most precise in his *Third Letter for Toleration,* in which, exasperated with an opponent's claim that "civil societies are instituted [by God] for attaining of all the benefits which civil society or political government can yield," Locke finally exclaims:

> If you will say, that commonwealths are not voluntary societies constituted by men, and by men freely entered into, I shall desire you to prove it.[119]

Locke's own discussion of the voluntary character of civil society as the *conditio sine qua non* of his contractarian model is focused upon the ways individuals enter and leave it. He begins by assuring his reader that "*Politick Societies* all *began* from a voluntary Union, and the mutual agreement of Men freely acting in the choice of their Governours, and forms of Government."[120] It could not be otherwise because political power, which distinguishes civil society from the state of nature, has its beginnings in a "Voluntary Agreement"[121] by its future subjects.[122]

Locke's position leads him to make a rigorous distinction between (1) the situation in which individuals give their "free consent," their "own consent," or in which they simply "willingly or of choice consent," and (2) the situation in which their consent is "forced" or "not freely" given, which causes a forced submission.[123] This differentiation—combined with the statement that a man's "Liberty of acting according to his own Will, is *grounded on* his having *Reason*"[124]—indicates once again that only a free individual is in a position to follow the law of nature. Locke's aim in drawing this distinction is to rest the voluntary adherence to civil society upon free consent and, consequently, to describe the institution of civil society as that which conforms to the law of nature and which thereby belongs to the normative part of his doctrine. The alternative is a non-voluntary state structure that is based upon forced submission. This non-voluntary state structure does not conform to the law of nature and, as such, is placed in the descriptive part of Locke's doctrine.[125]

Nevertheless, despite its unquestionable usefulness in rejecting natural political authority, this solution has a clear theoretical shortcoming. Referring to voluntary entrance into civil society, Locke claims that "This any number of Men may do, because it injures not the Freedom of the rest; they are left as they were in the Liberty of the State of Nature."[126] However, this might not always be the case.

To make this point clear I shall consider the situation of "independents," or those who prefer to stay in the state of nature rather than to join civil society.[127] If such an independent does business with a member of civil society and is wronged by that member, he faces two options. First, he might choose to take advantage of the civil society's judicial procedure. Second, he can reject this procedure and act on his own, which he has a perfect right to do as a person who remains in the state of nature with respect to civil society as a whole and each of its members. If he chooses the second option the civil society is entitled to force him to go along with its judicial arrangements, given its right to, as Locke puts it, "the defense of the Common-wealth from Foreign Injury."[128]

What is important here is the fact that the behavior of both sides—that of the independent and that of civil society—is legitimate according to the law of nature, the only system of norms that is common to them. Both sides exercise their powers—the individual executive power of the law of nature and the political power of civil society—in keeping with their rights of self-preservation. In both cases, the exercise of might is based upon right. Nevertheless, neither side has authorized the other to use its power;[129] hence, its use may be treated as based upon no right, but as pure coercion. Given the inequality between the might available to the independent and that available to civil society, Locke's claim that adherence to civil society is always based upon the free choice of individuals, understood as a decision made in the absence of coercion, cannot be true. Moreover, if the above analysis is correct, the distinction itself—which places free choice and voluntary adherence to civil society in the normative part of Locke's doctrine to oppose it to coercion, which belongs to the descriptive part—must be wrong. From the point of view of the independent, the force used against him by a legitimate civil society does not differ from the force used by a conqueror. The consequence of this shortcoming is very significant to the evaluation of the contractarian model of social relations offered in the *Two Treatises*. The contractarian model—despite Locke's efforts to prove the opposite—does not offer a perfect alternative to natural political authority.

The practical confirmation of the voluntary character of civil society is the positive-law guarantee of the natural right to leave the society under whose power one lives and to join or establish another one. Indeed, Locke assumes that in a well-ordered civil society the right to emigrate is justified. However, he does not treat it as an unconditional right. In light of his contractarian model, the endorsement of the right to emigrate is necessary; the reason for its conditional character creates a puzzle that is difficult for twentieth century interpreters to solve.

There is no doubt, states Locke, that people are "at Liberty to separate themselves from their Families, and the Government... and go and make distinct Common-wealths and other Governments." The question of emigration is not confined to the normative part of his doctrine, since "...there are no Examples so frequent in History, both Sacred and Prophane, as this of Men withdrawing themselves, and their Obedience, from the Jurisdiction they were born under."[130] Exercising the right to emigrate "has been the practice of the World from its first beginnings to this day." It concerns those who "are born under constituted and ancient Polities, that have established laws and set Forms of Government" as well as those who "were born in the Woods, amongst the unconfined Inhabitants that ran loose in them."[131]

The conditional character of the liberty to emigrate emerges when Locke presents the distinctions between tacit and express consent. He who has only tacitly consented, and who is willing to give up his possessions, is free to leave civil society at any time. On the other hand, he who has expressly consented to be a full member of civil society is always bound by his "positive Engagement," since in agreeing he gives up his right to emigrate. He "is perpetually and indispensably obliged to be and remain a Subject to it, and can never be again in the liberty of the state of nature." There are only two exceptions to this rule. The first is if the government is dissolved; the second is when the individual is granted permission to leave the country by the legitimate political authority.[132]

This insistence upon conditional emigration is an obvious contradiction in Locke's position.[133] To best understand him, it does not help to take the position of a twentieth century liberal and blame Locke for his practical restrictions on the right to emigrate—as some scholars tend to do[134]—rather, it is preferable to discuss this controversial solution with reference to his contractarian model and to its applicability in political practice.

There is no doubt that the restrictions Locke imposes upon the right to emigrate are in stark disagreement with his contractarian model. First, they contradict the logic of this model. The Lockean man enters civil society to have his natural rights preserved by the provisions of positive law.[135] However, in the case of emigration, the natural right of full members of civil society "to go and make distinct Common-wealths" is not preserved, but rather abolished by positive law. Second and more important, Locke's restrictions upon emigration undermine the very normative foundation of his contractarian model. The right to emigrate has a special, protective character with regard to other natural rights in civil society. The individual makes use of his right to emigrate when he comes to the conclusion that his other rights are not properly protected in a particular civil society.[136] When Locke deprives full members of civil society of this protective right, the only other protective right that they may make use of when they realize that their natural rights are not properly protected is the right to resist. Yet the fundamental difference between the right to emigrate and the right to resist is that, in the case of emigration, the individual alone makes the decision, while in the case of resistance the decision has to be made by the majority of civil society's members.[137] The collective decision to resist cannot replace the individual decision to emigrate. In Locke's contractarian model, each individual—whether in the state of nature or in civil society—is personally obliged to God to preserve his being and thus is responsible for his decisions concerning his preservation.[138] When Locke deprives the full members of civil society of the unconditional right to emigrate (and thereby deprives them of making a decision concerning their preservation in civil society) he undermines the normative link between man and God and therefore the normative foundation of his contractarian model.

Summary

My purpose in this chapter was to analyze and compare the position of the individual in the political structure in Filmer and Locke. I argued that in Filmer the status of the individual was that of subjection to paternal power. Filmer insisted that political power was derived from paternal power and as such it was unlimited; obedience to it was unconditional and adherence to the polity where it was exercised was compulsory. In rejecting these claims Locke indicated that the individual enjoyed the status of a member of civil society. This civic condition was characterized by the recognition of the individual as the only source of political power, the limited character of that power, the conditional character of political obligation and political legitimacy and, finally, the voluntary adherence to civil society.

The findings of this chapter fill a gap in Locke scholarship, which does not consider Locke's presentation of civil society as an element of his controversy with Filmer. Although some scholars, especially John Dunn, Richard Ashcraft, and Ruth Grant, considered certain issues presented in this chapter—such as the suicide taboo and the notions of consent and law[139]—as points Locke used in responding to Filmer, no one unified the separate issues, defining them as the constitutive principles of civil society. This failure is due to the absence in Locke scholarship of civil society as a Lockean category independent of and separate from the notion of government. In neglecting this category, interpreters of the *Two Treatises* have missed the crucial distinction between the civic condition (which was always carried by civil society) and mere allegiance to government (which sometimes included subjection to the absolute monarchy that Locke identified with the state of nature).[140] In turn, this neglect obscured the stark contrast between the Lockean individual as a member of civil society versus the Filmerian individual as subject of paternal power.

---

[1]Robert Filmer, "Directions for Obedience to Government in Dangerous or Doubtful Times," in Robert Filmer, *Patriarcha and Other Political Works of Sir Robert Filmer,* Peter Laslett, ed. (Oxford: Basil Blackwell, 1949), p. 232.

[2]Robert Filmer, "Anarchy of a Limited or Mixed Monarchy," in Robert Filmer, *Patriarcha and Other Political Works of Sir Robert Filmer,* Peter Laslett, ed. (Oxford: Basil Blackwell, 1949), p. 288-289.

[3]John Locke, *Two Treatises of Government,* Peter Laslett, ed. (Cambridge: Cambridge University Press, 1960), Second Treatise, §135.

[4]"True politicks I looke on as a Part of Moral Philosophie which is noething but the art of conducting men right in societie and supporting a communitie amongst its neighbours." Locke to Lady Peterborough (September/October, 1697) in E.S. de Beer, ed., *The Correspondence of John Locke* (Oxford: Clarendon Press, 1976), vol. VI, letter 2320, p. 215.

The Principles of Civil Society   95

⁵Filmer, "Directions for Obedience to Government," p. 233.
⁶John Locke, *Two Treatises of Government*, Peter Laslett, ed. (Cambridge: Cambridge University Press, 1960), First Treatise, §4.
⁷Locke, *Two Treatises of Government*, Second Treatise, §3.
⁸Ibid., §54.
⁹Ibid., §123.
¹⁰Ibid., §57.
¹¹Ibid., §128.
¹²Ibid., §§9, 13, 180.
¹³Ibid., §135.
¹⁴Ibid., §8.
¹⁵Ibid., §11.
¹⁶Ibid., §87.
¹⁷Ibid., §11.
¹⁸Ibid., §87
¹⁹Ibid., §11.
²⁰Ibid., §87.
²¹Ibid., §128.
²²Ibid., §87.
²³Ibid., §87.
²⁴Ibid., §131.
²⁵Ibid., §57.
²⁶Ibid., §87.
²⁷Ibid., §98, see also §§95, 96, 132, 87.
²⁸Ibid., §87.
²⁹Ibid., §95
³⁰Ibid., §129.
³¹Ibid., §171.
³²Ibid., §171. Locke confirms and elaborates on this position when he writes that individuals regain their two natural powers when they emigrate (Second Treatise, §121) and when civil society is "dissolved" (Locke, *Two Treatises of Government*, Second Treatise, §211).
³³Ibid., §127.
³⁴Filmer, "Anarchy of a Limited or Mixed Monarchy," p. 284.
³⁵Locke, *Two Treatises of Government*, Second Treatise, §130.
³⁶Ibid., §129.
³⁷Ibid., §168.
³⁸This assumption has been questioned by Windstrup, who treats Locke's prohibition of suicide as merely conditional. See George Windstrup, "Locke on Suicide," *Political Theory*, vol. 8, no. 2, (May 1980): 169-82. "Suicide," he claims, "if almost always immoral, is occasionally sanctioned by Lockean ethics." In reality, "Locke's showy insistence on his law of nature" is justified only by the needs of his political argument (ibid., p. 174). Windstrup draws this

conclusion from some statements in John Locke, *Essays on the Law of Nature* (Wolfgang von Leyden, ed. [Oxford: Clarendon Press, 1954], p. 173), where it is admitted that the "power of custom and of opinion" induces some men to "lay violent hands upon themselves and seek death as eagerly as others shun it"; and from John Locke, *Essay concerning Human Understanding* (Peter H. Niddhitch, ed. [Oxford, Clarendon Press, 1975], 2.22.54 and 2.22.66), where there are indications that men are more inclined to be persuaded by present pain than by future prospects of pleasure. It is therefore possible to claim that "suicide is altogether 'normal' for those subject to unremitting pain" (Windstrup, "Locke on Suicide," p. 172). Moreover, he also refers to the *Two Treatises,* indicating that individuals sometimes prefer to preserve their offspring rather than themselves (Locke, *Two Treatises of Government,* First Treatise, §56), and that a slave taken in a just war is in a position to resist the will of his master and to draw death on himself (Locke, *Two Treatises of Government,* Second Treatise, §23).

However, this evidence seems to miss the point; Windstrup considers examples from human behavior, which in Locke does not create ethical principles. What is right or wrong, as well as what is a right or duty of man, is determined by God's will (see ch. 2 above); the duty of self-preservation is specifically stated by the will of God (Locke, *Two Treatises of Government,* First Treatise, §86). Man's "strong desire of Preserving his Life and Being," on which Windstrup bases his line of argument, is "Planted in him" in order that he may easily follow the will of God (ibid.). If this desire ceases, its absence does not create a right that could oppose the duty imposed by God. It does not, therefore, weaken the normative strength of this duty in the cases discussed by Windstrup, including the last one. The last case—that of the slave who decides to terminate his slavery by death—does not help to reconcile a right to suicide with Locke's ethics, because the slave's choice is not founded upon any right. The slave lost all the rights of his previous moral status when he invaded the rights of others as an aggressor (in Locke, slavery is the price paid by an aggressor in the state of war). It is true that there is one passage in the Second Treatise—only mentioned by Windstrup but not discussed by him—which could suggest that the prohibition of suicide might have a conditional character. Locke writes in §6 that man "has not Liberty to destroy himself... but where some nobler use, than its bare Preservation calls for it." Nevertheless, this statement hangs in a doctrinal vacuum. Nowhere in the *Two Treatises* does Locke argue for any nobler use for one's life than its preservation. Compare Gary D. Glenn, "Inalienable Rights and Locke's Argument for Limited Government: Political Implications of Rights to Suicide," *The Journal of Politics,* vol. 46 (1984): 88-105, especially p. 85.

[39]Locke, *Two Treatises of Government,* Second Treatise, §6.
[40]Ibid., §23.
[41]Filmer, "Anarchy of a Limited or Mixed Monarchy," p. 285.

The Principles of Civil Society 97

[42] Locke, *Two Treatises of Government,* Second Treatise, §149. See also Glenn, "Inalienable Rights and Locke's Argument for Limited Government": 83-84.
[43] Locke, *Two Treatises of Government,* Second Treatise, §§6, 8, 128.
[44] Ibid., §9.
[45] Compare Wolfgang von Leyden, *Hobbes and Locke* (New York: St. Martin's Press, 1982) pp. 113-14.
[46] Locke, *Two Treatises of Government,* Second Treatise, §8.
[47] Ibid., §23.
[48] Ibid., §9.
[49] Ibid., §8.
[50] Filmer, "Anarchy of a Limited or Mixed Monarchy," p. 283.
[51] Filmer, "Patriarcha," p. 102.
[52] Locke, *Two Treatises of Government,* Second Treatise, §§22, 57, 59, 220.
[53] Ibid., §57.
[54] In the *Essays on the Law of Nature,* Locke defines law as "that which prescribes to everything the form and manner and measure of working," *Essays on the Law of Nature,* p. 117.
[55] Locke, *Two Treatises of Government,* Second Treatise, §57.
[56] Ibid., §63.
[57] Ibid., §57.
[58] Ibid., §22.
[59] Locke clearly owes the distinction between freedom and license to Aristotle. Among Locke's contemporaries this point is to be found in Milton. See John Milton, "The Tenure of Kings and Magistrates," Don M. Wolfe, ed., *Complete Prose Works of John Milton* (New Haven and London: Yale University Press, 1962), vol. III, p. 190.
[60] Locke, *Two Treatises of Government,* Second Treatise, §22.
[61] Compare Raymond Polin, "John Locke's Conception of Freedom," in J.W. Yolton, ed., *John Locke: Problems and Perspectives* (Cambridge: Cambridge University Press, 1969), p. 9.
[62] Locke, *Two Treatises of Government,* Second Treatise, §22.
[63] Ibid., §23.
[64] Ibid., §22.
[65] Ibid., §57.
[66] The only scholar who discusses Locke's presentation of freedom in the *Two Treatises* in terms of its two aspects, negative and positive, is Laslett, Introduction to the *Two Treatises,* p. 111. Tully, who has recently taken up this topic, denies that these two notions of liberty exist in Locke, as understood in Berlin's classic essay ("Two Concepts of Liberty," in Isaiah Berlin, *Four Essays on Liberty* [Oxford, Oxford University Press, 1969], pp. 118-172). Tully refers to Berlin's difficulty in classifying Locke as a representative of both the notion of negative and positive liberty ("Two Concepts," see pp. 124, 126, and 147).

He explains that "for Locke nothing is more important than 'positive' freedom because it is the means to salvation," James Tully, "Locke on Liberty," in Zbigniew Pelczynski and John Gray, eds., *Conceptions of Liberty in Political Philosophy* (London: Athlone Press, 1984), p. 71. However, this conclusion can only be reached through acceptance of Berlin's orthodoxy, which assumes that these two concepts cannot harmoniously co-exist in one system. Yet this is not the case in Locke; certainly the Lockean man needs positive freedom in order to reach salvation, but he cannot enjoy this positive liberty without the negative. Given Locke's account of the law of nature, his negative freedom is still in agreement with Berlin"s description of it as the area within which the subject is or should be left to do or to be what he is able to do or to be, without interference by other persons.

[67]Locke, *Two Treatises of Government*, Second Treatise, §137.

[68]Ibid., §137.

[69]Ibid., §§159, 160. For an illuminating discussion of the relationship between the law and royal prerogative in Locke, see von Leyden, *Hobbes and Locke*, pp. 145-46.

[70]Locke, *Two Treatises of Government*, Second Treatise, §210.

[71]Ibid., §164.

[72]Ibid., §159.

[73]Ibid.

[74]Ibid.

[75]The fact that individual natural rights, which constitute the moral basis for the political structure, cannot always be secured within this structure creates an obvious tension in Locke's doctrine. Some interpreters who clearly defend the heterogeneity of his political thought treat the natural rights of individuals as always inalienable and any governmental action against them as unjust. See C.E. Vaughan, *Studies in the History of Political Philosophy* (Manchester: Manchester University Press, 1825), vol. I, pp. 130-203; J.A. Smith, *The Growth and Decadence of Constitutional Government* (New York: Henry Holt, 1930), p. 4; and G.H. Sabine, *A History of Political Theory* (New York: Holt and Company, 1937), p. 529. Others, who find Locke consistent in this case and ascribe to him a homogeneous approach, see these rights as absorbed by and subordinated to the commonwealth. See Willmoore Kendall, *John Locke and the Doctrine of Majority Rule* (Urbane: University of Illinois Press, 1963), pp. 69, 72, 79, 90; C.B. Macpherson, *Political Theory of Possessive Individualism* (Oxford: Oxford University Press, 1962), pp. 214-15, 218, 231, 256-62; and Richard Cox, *Locke on War and Peace* (Oxford: Oxford University Press, 1960), pp. 115-23. A third group of interpreters (R.A. Goldwin, "John Locke," in Leo Strauss and Joseph Cropsey, eds., *History of Political Philosophy* [Chicago: Rand McNally and Company, 1963], pp. 453-54 and Glenn, "Inalienable Rights and Locke's Argument for Limited Government," pp. 100-102) stress these contradictions and treat them as an unresolved theoretical ten-

The Principles of Civil Society   99

sion which leaves room in political practice for action on either side (that of the individual and that of the commonwealth) based upon their respective calculation of how best to secure their respective rights.

All these interpretations are mistaken in that they neglect the deeply theological character of the law of nature—the foundation of the normative part of Locke's doctrine. First, given its imperative to preserve both individuals and society, the law of nature allows Locke to avoid the extreme solutions that the first two interpretations ascribe to him. Second, it makes it possible for him to justify the occasional sacrifice of individual rights to protect the rights of others, not in terms of utilitarian calculation, as the third interpretation seems to assume, but rather in terms of the God-imposed duty of the preservation of mankind.

[76] Locke, *Two Treatises of Government,* Second Treatise, §166.

[77] A discussion of Locke's royal prerogative is best understood when accompanied by a discussion of its tendency to corruption. Locke's anthropological beliefs, shaped by his historical observations, led him to conclude that there was a clear dependency between the extent of uncontrolled power and its corruption. Such power is liable to "flatter the Natural Vanity and Ambition of Men... apt of it self to grow and encrease with the Possession of any Power" (Locke, *Two Treatises of Government,* First Treatise §10). This rule concerns not only the power of the absolute monarch, which Locke treats as merely a physical capacity to use force (since, according to the principles of natural law, nobody can consent to it), but also the power of royal prerogative in civil society, to which that society's members gave up a part of their natural powers (Locke, *Two Treatises of Government,* Second Treatise §§162, 165, 166, 168). The power of royal prerogative, however, is limited in civil society by the public good, which can be achieved only when the natural rights of the citizens, specified in the act of social contract, are not transgressed by that power more than to a "tolerable degree" (Locke, *Two Treatises of Government,* Second Treatise §161). To keep the prerogative within proper limits, civil society must have at its disposal the whole machinery of civil government with the legislature at the head. Only in such circumstances can the people define, limit, and control the royal prerogative with positive laws, and in this way prevent it from becoming "an Arbitrary Power to do things harmful" to them (Locke, *Two Treatises of Government,* Second Treatise §§162,163). In other words, the power of royal prerogative, bearing the features of the power of an absolute monarch, may conform to the end of civil society only when it is or can be restrained by the civil government in which it is integrated. This position makes it clear that—contrary to some scholars' claims (see, most notably, Martin Seliger, *Liberal Politics of John Locke* [New York: Praeger 1968], pp. 247-250)—Locke does not leave any door open for an endorsement of absolute monarchy. The reason is quite simple: an introduction of absolutism would have proved incompatible with his contractarian model.

[78] Filmer, "Anarchy of a Limited or Mixed Monarchy," p. 284.
[79] Filmer, "Patriarcha," p. 62.
[80] This position prevails in Filmer's writings. For its occasional modification, see ch. 6 below.
[81] Locke, *Two Treatises of Government,* Second Treatise, §3.
[82] Locke's *Journal* for 15 July 1678, headed "Lex naturae" published in Wolfgang von Leyden, "John Locke and Natural Law," *Philosophy,* vol. XXXI (1956), p. 35.
[83] Locke, *Two Treatises of Government,* Second Treatise, §4.
[84] See Locke, *Essays on the Law of Nature,* pp. 161-69.
[85] Compare Laslett, "Introduction" in Locke, *Two Treatises of Government,* p. 84.
[86] See John Plamenatz, *Man and Society: Political and Social Theory* (New York: McGraw-Hill, 1963), vol. 1, pp. 221-40, especially p. 224; John W. Gough, *John Locke's Political Philosophy* (Oxford: Clarendon Press, 1973), pp. 52-79, especially p. 65; Hanna Pitkin, "Obligation and Consent," *American Political Science Review,* vol. LIX, no. 4 (1965): 990-9, vol. LX, no. 1 (1966), pp. 39-52. John Dunn, "Consent in the Political Theory of John Locke," *The Historical Journal,* vol. X, no. 2, (1968), pp. 153-82; and John Dunn, *Political Thought of John Locke* (Cambridge: Cambridge University Press, 1963), pp. 142-143.
[87] This is the conclusion drawn by Dunn; see his *Political Thought of John Locke,* p. 143.
[88] Locke, *Two Treatises of Government,* Second Treatise, §87.
[89] Ibid., §§197, 199.
[90] Ibid., §151.
[91] Commenting on Sherlock's position, which justified the government's right to subjects' obedience on the ground of its mere ability to exercise power (William Sherlock, *The Case of Allegiance due to Sovereign Powers* [London, 1691]) Locke wrote: "How long a month a year—or an hundred & by what rule what law of God. Long and short in such cases unless defined have no meaning people submit where they do not resist so that where there is no resistance there is a general submission, but there may be a general submission without a general consent which is an other thing." Cited in John Dunn, *Political Obligation in its Historical Context* (Cambridge: Cambridge University Press, 1980), p. 308.
[92] Robert Filmer, "Observations upon Aristotle's Politics," in Robert Filmer, *Patriarcha and Other Political Works of Sir Robert Filmer,* Peter Laslett, ed. (Oxford: Basil Blackwell, 1949), p. 226.
[93] Locke, *Two Treatises of Government,* Second Treatise, §119.
[94] Ibid., §122.
[95] This is Dunn's interpretation. That Locke might have had in mind real events as constituting express consent, see Dunn, "Consent in the Political

Theory of John Locke," p. 168.

[96]Russell refers to Thomas Hobbes' *Leviathan* (ed. C.B. Macpherson [Harmondsworth: Penguin, 1985], Chs. XIV, XXI) and to Samuel Pufendorf's *De Iure Naturae et Gentium* ([Oxford: Clarendon Press, 1934], 3.6.1; 3.6.2). See Paul Russell, "Locke on express and tacit consent," *Political Theory,* vol. 14, no.2 (May 1986): 291-306, especially pp. 292-96.

[97]See Dunn, "Consent in the Political Theory of John Locke," pp. 167-68.

[98]Locke, *Two Treatises of Government,* Second Treatise, §116, 117.

[99]Ibid., §119.

[100]Ibid., §121.

[101]Ibid., §119.

[102]In contrast, Geraint Parry claims that "the only instance of tacit consent which Locke supplies is that given by foreigners who settle in or visit a country." See Geraint Parry, *John Locke* (London: George Allen & Unwin, 1978), p. 107. Other scholars overemphasize one sort of performance as typical of tacit consent. For example, Dunn suggests that "the persons of whom the category is predicated at all specifically appear mostly to be resident or transient aliens," Dunn, *Political Thought of John Locke,* pp. 131-32; see also Russell, "Locke on express and tacit consent," p. 297, where he assumes that "Locke regards the possession of land as a paradigm case of tacit consent."

[103]Locke, *Two Treatises of Government,* Second Treatise, §121.

[104]Considering the aim of Locke's distinction between express and tacit consent, it is difficult to believe that his real intention was to indicate a necessary link between citizenship and the ownership of land. Apart from the sole example of the aforementioned §116 of the Second Treatise, the rest of his discourse does not give any convincing textual evidence which could support such an interpretation. In Locke, citizenship is not a requirement for the tenure of land (as Vaughan argues in his *Studies in the History of Political Philosophy,* vol. I, p. 191); nor is the possession of land assumed to be a requirement of citizenship (as Macpherson believes, misinterpreting §120 of the Second Treatise—see his *Political Theory of Possessive Individualism,* pp. 249-251. For a criticism of Macpherson's position, see Dunn, "Consent in the Political Theory of John Locke," pp. 165-66 and Russell, "Locke on Express and Tacit Consent," p. 298).

[105]Filmer, "Patriarcha," p. 82.

[106]Filmer, "Observations upon Aristotle's Politics," p. 211.

[107]Filmer, "Anarchy of a Limited or Mixed Monarchy," p. 285.

[108]Robert Filmer, "Observations on Mr. Hobbes's Leviathan," in Robert Filmer, *Patriarcha and Other Political Works of Sir Robert Filmer,* Peter Laslett, ed. (Oxford: Basil Blackwell, 1949), p. 243.

[109]Filmer, "Anarchy of a Limited or Mixed Monarchy," p. 286.

[110]Locke, *Two Treatises of Government,* Second Treatise, §96.

[111]Ibid., §97.

[112] Ibid., §98.
[113] Ibid., §98.
[114] Ibid., §98.
[115] Ibid., §96.
[116] Ibid., §95.
[117] Filmer, "Anarchy of a Limited or Mixed Monarchy," p. 286.
[118] Filmer, "Observations upon H. Grotius De Jure belli et Pacis," p. 273.
[119] John Locke, "A Third Letter for Toleration," in John Locke *The Works of John Locke* (London, 1823), vol. VI, p. 212.
[120] Locke, *Two Treatises of Government*, Second Treatise, §102.
[121] Ibid., § 173.
[122] Ibid., §179.
[123] Ibid., §§102, 112, 173, 175, 176, 192, 198.
[124] Ibid., §63
[125] The best example of such a nonvoluntary state structure is that of absolute monarchy, which Locke identifies with the (ordinary) state of nature. See Locke, *Two Treatises of Government*, Second Treatise, § 90.
[126] Ibid, §95.
[127] For a discussion of the situation of "independents" stated in terms of civil society's right of self-defense, see Robert Nozick, *Anarchy, State, and Utopia* (New York: Basic Books, 1974), pp. 54-119.
[128] Locke, *Two Treatises of Government*, Second Treatise, §3.
[129] The fact that "independents" and civil society remain in the state of nature rules out such an authorization. To analyze their mutual relationship in terms of "legitimate political power" or "political authority"—as does Daniel Farrell in his "Coercion, Consent, and the Justification of Political Power: A New Look at Locke's Consent Claim," *Archiv fuer Rechts-und Sozialphilosophie* (vol. LXV no. 4 [1979], pp. 521-540), is therefore not in agreement with the premises of the *Two Treatises*.
[130] Locke, *Two Treatises of Government*, Second Treatise, §115.
[131] Ibid., §116.
[132] Ibid., §121.
[133] This contradiction is noted by Kendall, *John Locke and the Doctrine of Majority Rule*, p. 79; Seliger, *Liberal Politics of John Locke*, pp. 278-80; and Dunn, *Political Thought of John Locke*, p. 133.
[134] Kendall, as in *John Locke and the Doctrine of Majority Rule* (p. 79, fn. 71) and Seliger, in *Liberal Politics of John Locke* (pp. 282-83) seem to take this approach.
[135] See Dunn, *Political Thought of John Locke,* p. 133, who, with reason, states that the right to leave the country is not "a right, a title which [the subjects] could justly claim in their own person against the sovereign."
[136] . See ch. 5.
[137] Locke, *Two Treatises of Government*, Second Treatise, §96-98 in connec-

tion with §209, 243.

[138]For further discussion of this point, see ch. 5.

[139]Dunn, *Political Thought of John Locke,* pp. 88-89; Richard Ashcraft, *Locke's Two Treatises of Government* (London: Allen & Unwin, 1987), pp. 157-160; and Ruth W. Grant, *John Locke's Liberalism* (Chicago and London: The University of Chicago Press, 1987), pp. 78-79.

[140]Locke, *Two Treatises of Government,* Second Treatise, §90.

Chapter 5

The Position and Structure of Civil Government

Thus far we have analyzed the manner in which Filmer and Locke constructed the first two elements of their models. Each thinker introduced his first element—paternal power or superhuman agency (H^1) and individual or human agency (C^1), equipped them with their own standards of rationality, then applied them to the particular issue of property. In presenting the second element of his model, each thinker described the relations among individuals: Filmer described them as created and defined by paternal power and reflecting its standards of rationality (H^2); Locke defined them as created and defined by individual agents while reflecting their standards of rationality (C^2). We can now continue our discussion by considering the third element of their models—the relations between individuals and their government (H^3 and C^3). Filmer maintains, as we may now expect, that these relations are created and defined by paternal power and reflect its standards of rationality; Locke describes them as created and defined by individual agents and reflecting their standards of rationality.

In this chapter I shall analyze the position of paternal power in the Filmerian polity and civil government in Lockean civil society. I shall argue that Filmer's position implies three basic claims: paternal power is itself the highest terrestrial end; this end is implemented by the presence of its subjects; and, finally, it is implemented because the subjects remain in full dependency upon that power. Locke argues for fundamental alternatives to each of Filmer's claims. It is the individual and his well-being, Locke says, that is the highest terrestrial end; the ends of individuals in civil society are implemented by the presence of civil government; and these ends are implemented because civil government remains fully dependent upon civil society. Locke presents the dependency of civil government upon civil society in his detailed discussion of sovereignty, political trusteeship, and the structure of that government.

Filmer's fundamental claim, basic not only to his notion of government but also to his entire holistic model, is that paternal power is the highest terrestrial end. Indeed, paternal power is initially established by God in Paradise[1] as "the only right and natural authority of a supreme Father." Since then, it has continued thus and "always shall be continued to the end of the world."[2] As an end in itself, paternal power is independent of the existence of its subjects. Filmer writes that, as soon as Adam was created, he "was monarch of the world, though he had no subjects; for though there could not be actual government until there were subjects, yet by the right of nature it was to Adam to be governor of his posterity: though not in act, yet at least in habit."[3]

Of course, Filmer's system does have something to say about the status of subjects. Filmer does discuss the relation between the members of civil society—or as he preferred to call them, the "multitude" or people—and paternal power. This relation can be convincingly described as one-way, three-dimensional dependency. First, the dependency is conceptual. "Since civil society cannot be imagined without power of government,"[4] the end of the subjects' existence is exclusively an attribute of paternal power, derived from the end of paternal power itself. Second, the dependency is moral. Preservation of the people is justified because paternal power needs them. Filmer argues along this line when he rejects Aristotle's conception of tyranny. On his view, a tyrannical government that destroys its people is a fiction, since without the people no government could exercise its power; to enjoy its power, the government has to preserve its people rather than destroy them. Indeed, Filmer assures his reader that,

> The truth of this strongly proves, that it is in nature impossible to have a form of government that can be for destruction of a people, as tyranny is supposed; if we will allow people to be governed, we must grant, they must in the first place be preserved, or else they cannot be governed.[5]

Third, the dependency is normative. The holder of paternal power sets up rules according to which the people should live their lives as subjects of that power.[6]

Thus, in Filmer's presentation of the position of paternal power in the polity there are three basic claims. Paternal power is itself the highest terrestrial end; this end is implemented by the presence of its subjects; and it is implemented by their presence because they remain in full dependency upon paternal power.

To Filmer's assertion that paternal power is itself the highest terrestrial end, Locke answers that it is the individual and his well-being that is such an end. Where Filmer claims that the end of paternal power is implemented by the presence of its subjects, Locke claims that the ends of individuals in civil society are implemented by the presence of civil government. Where Filmer insists that the end of paternal power is implemented by the presence of its subjects because they remain in full dependency upon that power, Locke maintains that the ends of individuals in civil society are implemented by the presence of civil government because civil government remains fully dependent upon civil society.

Locke's discussion of the law of nature, the state of nature, property, and civil society can safely be treated as his detailed demonstration of how God's (and thus man's) ends are, or at least should be, made concrete. As a cognitive being provided by his Maker with reason, man is able to know the principles of the law of nature. His first lesson from the law of nature is that God's aim concerning the human race is its preservation. The duty imposed by God—that of the self-preservation of each individual and that of the preservation of mankind—ensures that God's appointed end becomes the goal of man. Moreover, since God has given man physical strength and equipped him with the two natural powers, he can also execute the provisions of natural law. Thus, man is sufficiently prepared for pursuing his end.

As God achieves his end for mankind through the individual, the individual accomplishes his end by means of civil society. As the goal of man (the preservation of himself and the rest of mankind) is not autonomous but rather originates in the goal of God, so the public good (the promotion of which is the task of civil society) is not an end in itself but a transposition of the individual goals of its members. Civil society is prepared for the achievement of this end, since the individual has provided it with political power—just as he himself has been equipped by God with the two natural powers to implement God's end.

Such implementation is possible at every level of Locke's model. In the natural order, God's ends are fulfilled by individuals who make use of their natural powers. In the conventional order, civil society implements the ends of the individuals, first by protecting them from each other, and second, in extreme situations, by protecting itself against uncivil government through its use of political power. In such situations, "People have a Right to act as Supreme [power], and continue the Legislative in themselves."[7] However, the ends of the individuals are usually best pursued in the conventional order by civil government.

Locke's inclusion of an argument for the development of civil society and civil government is necessary because without them there is a lack of efficiency in meeting man's goal. Indeed, the individual in the state of nature cannot implement his ends very efficiently. Civil society can do it better than the individual in the state of nature and civil government, which has at its disposal the powers of the legislative, executive, federative, and royal prerogative, can do it even better than civil society.

Thus, the outline of the ways in which God's and man's ends are implemented illustrates that Locke's argument implies an interaction of two hierarchies—that of ends and that of efficiency in their implementation. The first hierarchy leads from God's end down to that of man, then to that of civil society and lastly to that of civil government. The relation among the links of this hierarchy may be considered as a one-way, three-dimensional dependency. It is conceptual, because the reason for the existence of each lower link in the hierarchy originates in the next higher link. Thus, the end of civil government reaches back to that of civil society, that of civil society to that of man, that of man to that of God. The dependency is also moral for similar reasons: the existence of each lower link in the hierarchy is justified only by reference to the next higher one. It is likewise a normative dependency, since the person or institution that represents each higher link in the hierarchy sets up the rules according to which the representative of the lower link should implement his ends. Thus, God determines the way in which man implements his human end, man determines the way in which civil society's end is to be implemented, and civil society determines the way civil government's end is to be implemented.

The second hierarchy, that of efficiency in implementing these ends, leads conversely from civil government down through civil society to the individual. Indeed, civil government has at its disposal such institutions as the legislative, the executive, the federative, and the power of royal prerogative, which specialize in implementing the public good and is thus best prepared to do so. Civil society, when it acts alone and not through its civil government—as, for example, when it launches resistance—is less efficient in implementing that good. Nevertheless, it is sufficiently prepared to carry out this task since it has at its disposal the political power of the commonwealth[8] and is led by its majority. The individual in the state of nature is less efficient in his efforts to preserve himself and other human beings than are civil society and civil government since he has at his disposal only his two natural powers.

The relation between the corresponding links of the two hierarchies is inversely proportional. In the hierarchy of ends the goal of human self-preservation is the highest terrestrial end, but the capacity of every individual to implement this end by himself is the weakest in the hierarchy of efficiency. Similarly, in the hierarchy of ends the purpose of civil government takes the lowest place, but in the hierarchy of efficiency the position of government is the strongest.

Analyzing this inversely proportional relation shows that by introducing these two hierarchies into his model, Locke managed to create a construction which guarantees that the individual's end, the highest terrestrial end, could be implemented in the most efficient way. This was accomplished without weakening the dependency resulting from the hierarchy of ends. This achievement, which is already visible in the relation between the individual and civil society, becomes even more important when Locke considers the bonds between civil society and civil government. The dependency of civil government upon civil society is expanded in Locke's concepts of sovereignty and trust, and is combined with the principle of efficiency in his discussion of the structure of civil government. I shall now move to a detailed presentation of these concepts.

In the *Two Treatises*, Locke does not use the term "sovereignty" in spelling out his own doctrine; instead, he discusses the term only as it is defined by Filmer,[9] who considers it "unlimited and undivided" authority.[10] Since he accepts Filmer's definition of the term, he never uses it in his own normative doctrine—where there is no room for sovereignty so understood. Nevertheless, the notion of sovereignty is present in Locke's system.[11] Locke's use of the notion reflects some crucial elements of Bodin's classic definition of "sovereignty' as stated in the *Methodus*.[12] In fact, in his argument against Filmer, Locke mentions two such attributes or "marks of sovereignty," namely, the power to sentence transgressors to death and to declare war and peace. Moreover, an analysis of the two natural powers of individuals in the state of nature and of political power in civil society indicates that other such attributes of sovereignty as defined by Bodin (especially the authority to legislate) are to be found in Locke's system. The important point is, however, that in Locke's system—unlike in Filmer's—sovereignty is neither unlimited nor undivided. Indeed, it is limited by the imperative of the preservation of mankind. It is also divided, since, as shall be shown below, it simultaneously resides partly in individuals, partly in civil society, and partly in civil government (and eventually in different parts of that government).

There is no doubt that in the state of nature the Lockean man is sovereign. This is so because he is responsible to God for implementing the end that is both his and God's: the preservation of himself and his fellow men. What is special about his sovereignty in the state of nature is that he himself enjoys the attributes of sovereignty; when he enters civil society, he transfers these attributes of sovereignty to it. Having them at its disposal, civil society implements its end—the public good—which is a transposition of the ends of individuals in the state of nature. In spite of this arrangement, however, each member of civil society, as an individual, is still personally responsible to God for the implementation of his individual ends by civil society. Because of this non-transferable responsibility, he may not renounce his attributes of sovereignty irreversibly. If civil society fails to implement his individual ends, he must be in a position to carry on with this task by himself. He cannot dissolve civil society, since it is not established by him alone and does not exist only to implement his individual ends. He can, however, make use of his right to emigrate—a right which, though vaguely and confusingly stated, Locke admits. In this way, a member of civil society returns to the state of nature, from which he can join another civil society; to do this, he needs to have his attributes of sovereignty returned to him. Thus, it is not an exaggeration to conclude that a member of civil society does not cease to be sovereign, in spite of the fact that he cannot make use of the attributes of sovereignty that he enjoyed in the state of nature. Indeed, he judges by himself which civil society to join and for how long; in other words, he is always in a position to decide when and where he should suspend his own use of his attributes of sovereignty and authorize civil society to use them, and when and where he should withdraw this authorization.

The conceptual relations between a sovereign individual and a sovereign civil society are duplicated in Locke's presentation of the dependency of civil government upon civil society. Civil society is sovereign when it implements its end, the public good, before the establishment of civil government and after its dissolution.[13] The only limits upon the

"Supreme Power" of civil society result from the sovereignty of its members. In turn, when civil government is in office, civil society transfers to that government its attributes of sovereignty; but it is still a sovereign body, since, as Locke puts it, "there remains still *in the People a Supream Power* to remove or *alter the Legislative*"[14] which is the foundation of civil government. The reasoning behind Locke's position is fairly clear. Transferring the attributes of sovereignty does not mean transferring the responsibility for the task that is carried out with these attributes. Since "God and Nature" never allow either a man or the body of the people "to neglect his own preservation,"[15] the community "perpetually *retains a Supream Power* of saving themselves from the attempts and designs of any Body."[16]

The question of civil society's responsibility for implementing the public good is not stated by Locke very precisely, but it is sufficiently visible to be considered a basis for the sovereignty of that body. The dependency resulting from the hierarchy of ends, which leads from God and his end through those of man and civil society to civil government, is accompanied by a chain of responsibility for implementing those ends. Given the considerations presented up to this point, it is clear that in this chain, the individual is responsible to God and civil government to civil society.

As regards civil society, there is also little doubt that it is responsible for its task; however, a practical question arises when one considers to whom this body as a whole owes its responsibility. Locke's suggestion that responsibility is owed directly to "God and Nature" is to the point as long as civil society is treated as the sum of the individuals who are its members. But this does not explain much, because it is still an individual that is responsible to God, just as in the state of nature. The answer then, in keeping with Locke's notion of dependency resulting from the hierarchy of ends, is that civil society owes its responsibility to its individual members. The other question that arises here concerns the sanction backing up the particular responsibilities of civil society. In the case of the individual, it is the prospect of punishment in the terrestrial world or the life hereafter that backs up the provisions of natural law; in the case of civil government, it is the prospect of its dissolution. The only sanction against civil society available to its individual member is, again, the exercise of his right to emigrate—a right which, despite imposing upon it all previously discussed limitations, Locke admits.

Thus, civil society's responsibility to implement its members' individual ends by promoting the public good means that the sovereignty of that body does not cease when this aim is carried out by a civil government. Accordingly, civil society retains the right to dissolve one government and to appoint another, the form and personnel of which society may decide on its own.[17] Moreover, it unequivocally follows from the one-way dependency of civil government upon civil society that this society, in making the decision to dissolve the government, is absolutely independent of—and sovereign over—the behavior of the government. Even if civil government carries out its task properly, it cannot prevent civil society from dissolving it if this society finds such a course of action right. Civil society does not share its responsibility to its members with civil government; therefore, it cannot share this decision with the government either. As Locke puts it, in this case none but *"The People shall be Judge."*[18]

Apart from sovereignty, the concept of trust also reflects the Lockean dependency of civil government upon civil society. Locke treats the power of the legislative, which is the foundation of all government, as "only a Fiduciary Power to act for certain ends."[19] These ends are that "men might have and secure *their Properties.*"[20] He insists that the members of civil society have a right "to remove or *alter the Legislative*, when they find the *Legislative* act contrary to the trust reposed in them."[21] Thus, it is left to civil society to decide whether any part of the government acts contrary to its trust; "for who shall be Judge whether his Trustee or Deputy acts well, and according to the Trust resposed in him, but he who deputes him, and must, by having deputed him have still a Power to discard him, when he fails in his Trust?"[22]

In discussing Locke's use of the concept of trust in the context of civil government's dependency upon civil society, it is very difficult not to treat it as his application of a private-law metaphor to politics. Such a legal understanding of this notion, stated very forcefully by Sir Ernest Barker and J.W. Gough,[23] is indeed extremely illuminating insofar as such an understanding makes it possible to avoid interpreting the relation between civil society and civil government in terms of the classic contract of government—and, thereby, insofar as it excludes any notion of equality between them. Such an understanding of trust rejects any suggestion of mutuality of rights and duties on both sides. If civil society is treated as a subject that combines in itself the position due in private law to the creator of the trust (the truster) and at the same time, to the beneficiary of the trust—while the position of the trustee is left to civil government—then all the rights connected with their relation are allotted to civil society, while all the duties are left to civil government.

The Position and Structure of Civil Government

In light of civil government's position in the hierarchy of ends discussed above, there is no doubt that Locke would have accepted and justified the conclusions reached with this legal interpretation. However, he would have pointed at the concept of trust as an expression of the dependency of civil government upon civil society, rather than as the origin of that dependency. But, while it is true that Locke's contemporaries used trust as a category that focused on a ruler's responsibility to serve the public good, a responsibility they traced back to the dependency of the trustee upon the truster, they did not always imply the same political position as that taken by Locke. On the one hand, the royalists used this metaphor to indicate the responsibility of the monarch treated as a trustee exclusively of God, his truster. On the other hand, the supporters of limited government adopted it and stressed not so much its legal character but rather its general meaning, which expressed a moral bond between a ruler and his subjects. Thus, when Locke introduced the concept of trust into his discourse (just as with the concept of sovereignty), he was by no means adopting an idea with clear political connotations that would shape his doctrine accordingly.[24] On the contrary, he gave to these two popular and ambiguous concepts a meaning very specific to his own argument.

Accordingly, the notion of trust treated exclusively as a legal metaphor—as it is by Barker and Gough—no matter how important to the expression of the dependency of civil government upon civil society, neither explains the full relation between these two institutions nor captures the whole conceptual scope which Locke connected with that notion. What prevails in his thinking is the moral dimension of trust, which is attributed not to the conventional but to the natural order. In Locke's view, trust does not arise from dependency created by man, nor is it followed by sanctions imposed by man for its breach. The duty to be trustworthy is set up by God as a provision of the law of nature: faith "and keeping of Faith belongs to Men, as Men, and not as Members of Society."[25] That the sanction for neglecting the duty to be trustworthy, as with every sanction of the natural law, is to be expected more in the next life than in this terrestrial life, does not weaken the deity's extraordinary normative force. As Locke insists, "The Obligations of that Eternal Law... are so great, and so strong, in the case of *Promises*, that Omnipotency it self can be tyed by them."[26] The reason for this insistence is transparent: trustworthiness is both the constitutive virtue of, and the key causal condition for the very existence and preservation of any human society; mankind can survive only as a community if it is composed of moral, trustworthy, rational agents.[27] One's duty to be trustworthy is followed by the duty to trust others;[28] these duties apply to everyone, ruled and rulers alike. Thus, they also extend to the relation between civil society and its government, especially to the power of the royal prerogative. The bond between the holder of the prerogative and civil society cannot be treated entirely as that between the trustee and his truster, as in the legal metaphor, since the monarch directly executes the law of nature and thereby remains in some way in the state of nature toward the members of civil society.

But Locke's concept of trust plays a further role in illuminating the relation between civil society and its government. When Locke states in the normative part of his doctrine the duty to trust human beings, he does not draw any distinction between rulers and the ruled. Nevertheless, in the descriptive part of his doctrine he discusses factors that prevent people from being trustworthy and his anthropological beliefs, shaped by the historical observations,[29] lead him to the conclusion that holders of power are more vulnerable to corruption (and thus less trustworthy) than their fellow human beings. This conclusion is the key to understanding the bond between civil society and civil government, as expressed in terms of the concept of trust.

Thus, the bond under discussion can be described as follows: Civil government is a trustee of civil society, upon which it remains in normative dependency. The members of civil society have to trust their rulers as they do all other human beings, in order not to render impossible the implementation of their end, the preservation of civil society, which is carried out by the government. However, as rational beings they have to remember that their trustees, precisely because of the position that they occupy to carry out that task, cannot be as trustworthy as others.[30]

Locke does not discuss the dependency of civil government upon civil society solely in terms of the concepts of sovereignty and trust. Rather, he proceeds to consider the inner structure of civil government in terms of both its efficiency and its dependency upon civil society. Before analyzing this structure, I shall briefly outline Filmer's position on the form of government that Locke rejected in his own presentation.

Filmer's account of the form of government may be seen in two ways. Taking a pragmatic viewpoint, one could conclude that, given the polemical core of his writings, he treated this problem as irrelevant. Since "all power on earth is either derived or usurped from the fatherly power," and since that power always requires the same obedience, there is no difference between, for example, the monarchy of Charles I and

Cromwell's republic. To take this viewpoint, however, would be to interpret the issue from the point of view of the subjects of paternal power; it would be to base the discussion of the form of government on an analysis of the condition of the individuals over whom paternal power was exercised.

But this is not Filmer's approach. It is true that he pressed this point very strongly upon his reader, but this was only an indirect result of his holistic model, and not its goal.[31] Filmer discussed the form of government from the point of view of paternal power itself, and thus he was concerned with the conditions in which such power could be exercised. What he wanted to achieve above all was an application of paternal power to politics that would preserve it in the same form in which Adam had exercised it.[32] Thus, Filmer could announce with confidence against the whole Aristotelian tradition, "there is no form of government but monarchy only,"[33] by which he understood only absolute monarchy. What led him to this bold conclusion was his discussion of paternal power in terms of the will of its holder.[34] In his view, for any government to do anything, it had to act with a single will, since Adam, the sole original holder of paternal power, had exercised it exclusively according to his own will. Filmer treated absolute monarchy as the only form of government, simply because only in absolute monarchy could the "single will" condition be met; only in absolute monarchy could the "perfection and permanence" of paternal power, exercised by the single will, be expressed and preserved. Having reached this conclusion, Filmer did not suggest that other forms of government were inefficient or illegitimate but that they could hardly be considered government,[35] because no proper institution of government existed in them. He did admit that in different regimes "some small show of government" was to be found, but, he added, these remained "poor and beggarly."[36] What allowed them to exercise their power at all was "borrowed or patched up of a broken and distracted monarchy."[37]

Locke's discussion of the form of government consists of two stages. The first stage gives the wrong impression—that this issue is irrelevant to his contractarian model. The only point that he presses upon his reader in the first stage is the belief that whatever the sort of government, it must be found fit and chosen by the people.[38] Accordingly, wherever their majority decides to place the power of making laws—whether in one person (monarchy), in a few (oligarchy, which Locke calls aristocracy), or in the community (democracy)—all these forms of government can serve the end of civil society and promote the public good the same way.³⁹ However, in the second stage of his discussion, when he goes on to consider the structure of government, he does not confirm his previous statement that each of these classic forms can equally suit his purpose. In fact, they cannot do so because it is impossible to create within the framework of each of them a balance of power between the legislative and the executive, which would ensure the dependency of civil government upon civil society.⁴⁰

Balancing the power of government depends upon "placing several parts of it in different hands."⁴¹ The first and most important step in this direction is the separation of the executive from the legislative. This move results from Locke's realization that it is,

> a temptation to human frailty apt to grasp at Power, for the same Persons who have the Power of making Laws, to have also in their hands the power to execute them, whereby they may exempt themselves from Obedience to the Laws they make, and suit the Law, both in its making and execution, to their own private advantage, and thereby come to have a distinct interest from the rest of the Community, contrary to the end of Society and Government.⁴²

This separation of powers is the precondition of the establishment of civil government, since as long as these two powers are not placed in different persons or bodies, a regime (such as absolute monarchy) remains in the state of nature toward its subjects.⁴³

However, even if holders of legislative and executive power are distinct, in exercising these powers they are likely to follow their own interests and not that of civil society. Locke's second step in preventing them from doing so is the introduction of constitutional solutions that require their interaction. These solutions are based upon two canons of Locke's constitutional thinking: the superiority of the legislative to all other powers, and the inseparability of the executive from the power of the royal prerogative.

In every well-ordered commonwealth based upon the rule of law, the legislative is the holder of the supreme power by virtue of its lawmaking.⁴⁴ As such, it not only controls but also creates all subsequent inferior powers, including the executive. For example, in a constitutional arrangement in which the executive has no role in the lawmaking process, it "is visibly subordinate and accountable to it [the legislative], and may be at pleasure changed and displaced."⁴⁵ However, this is not the situation in which Locke is interested. Rather, he gives this example to stress the general rule of the supremacy of the legislative.⁴⁶

The Position and Structure of Civil Government   117

What Locke discusses at length and what forms a crucial point in his presentation of civil government is another constitutional arrangement, whereby the legislative, in spite of its theoretical supremacy in relation to the executive, is unable to remove the executive from power. In this situation a monarch who, exercising the executive power, also has a share in the legislative process and can exercise a veto over legislation, "is no more subordinate [to the legislative] than he himself shall think fit, which one may certainly conclude will be but very little."[47] Thus, by virtue of his position, the monarch can ensure that the legislative, as every other body in the commonwealth, will remain subject to the law. Locke recommends that the legislative power should be placed not "in one lasting Assembly always in being, or in one Man,"[48] but rather "wholly or in part, in Assemblies which are variable, whose Members upon the Dissolution of the Assembly, are Subjects under the common Laws of their Country, equally with the rest."[49] Accordingly, as a person almost independent from the legislative body, the monarch is entrusted—if other constitutional solutions are not preferable—with the power of assembling and dismissing it,[50] and even with the task of reforming the franchise by creating new constituencies in place of boroughs whose populations have diminished.[51]

Both of these functions of the monarch are expressly justified by referring to his position as holder of the royal prerogative. Nevertheless, Locke confuses the whole question of the balance of powers within civil government when he claims that the monarch is entitled to carry out electoral reforms as the executive head. This claim creates a problem that Locke considers "incapable of a remedy." He presents the problem as a contradiction between two claims. The first is that neither any power inferior to the legislative body nor even civil society itself can alter that legislative body so long as civil government remains. The second claim is that, in constitutional practice, it may be necessary for such alterations by the executive, which nevertheless always remains inferior to the legislative.

To solve this problem, Locke escapes into fiction and assures his reader that the reform of the franchise "cannot be judg'd, to have set up a new Legislative, but to have restored the old and true one."[52] Of course, Locke solves here a problem of his own making.[53] However, it is worth mentioning that, contrary to Locke's assertions, this problem does not exist, because it simply cannot arise in his doctrine. The whole confusion must be ascribed to Locke's astonishing failure—and indeed to that of some of his interpreters[54]—to draw the obvious distinction between the normative status of the monarch as head of the executive and as holder of the royal prerogative. In the first case, he acts exclusively as the executor of positive law and thus cannot alter the legislative, which is the source of that law. However, in the second case, he is a trustee of civil society and acts only according to the law of nature. Thus, he is at liberty to alter the legislative in accordance with natural law—a law which, as Locke states, "is to govern even the legislative itself."[55]

Summary

In this chapter, I analyzed the relations between paternal power and its subjects in Filmer and the relation between civil society and civil government in Locke. The essential quality pervading these relations is that of dependency: in Filmer's case, dependency of the subjects on paternal power; in Locke's case dependency of civil government on civil society, a dependency that he justifies by introducing the concepts of sovereignty, political trusteeship, and the structure of civil government.

Although the dependency of rulers on the ruled is a commonplace in scholarship, the relation between civil society and civil government has not been duly discussed in the context of Locke's controversy with Filmer. Indeed, in approaching this issue most commentators, including Julian Franklin, Martin Seliger, and Ruth Grant, have limited themselves to observing that Locke's notion of popular sovereignty is a direct rejection of Filmer's position.[56] Missing is a comprehensive discussion of all the concepts and devices, including sovereignty, political trusteeship, and the structure of civil government, all of which Locke uses to illustrate the dependency of civil government on civil society. This state of affairs is a consequence of other more general failures in Locke scholarship, such as the previously mentioned absence of a complete analysis of the relation between civil society and civil government as categories independent of and separate from each other,[57] and even the denial of the existence of civil society without civil government.[58]

---

[1]Robert Filmer, "Discourse, quoted in Gordon G. Schochet, *Patriarchalism in Political Thought* (Oxford: Basil Blackwell, 1975), pp. 47-48.

[2]Robert Filmer, "Patriarcha," in Robert Filmer, *Patriarcha and Other Political Works of Sir Robert Filmer,* Peter Laslett, ed. (Oxford: Basil

Blackwell, 1949), p. 62.

[3]Robert Filmer, "The Anarchy of a Limited or Mixed Monarchy," in Robert Filmer, *Patriarcha and Other Political Works of Sir Robert Filmer,* Peter Laslett, ed. (Oxford: Basil Blackwell, 1949), p. 289.

[4]Ibid., pp. 289-90.

[5]Robert Filmer, "Observations upon Mr. Milton Against Salamasus," in Peter Laslett, *Patriarcha and Other Political Works of Sir Robert Filmer,* Peter Laslett, ed. (Oxford: Basil Blackwell, 1949), p. 259.

[6]For example, see Filmer, "Patriarcha," pp. 102-103, 105-106.

[7]John Locke, *Two Treatises of Government,* Peter Laslett, ed. (Cambridge: Cambridge University Press, 1960), Second Treatise, §243.

[8]In ch. 6, I discuss at length the manner in which political power, as a result of resistance, returns to the people to be subsequently used against the rulers.

[9]John Locke, *Two Treatises of Government,* Peter Laslett, ed. (Cambridge: Cambridge University Press, 1960), First Treatise, §§64-68, 75-76, 129, 130-131, 133; Second Treatise, §§83, 108, 115.

[10]John Locke, *Two Treatises of Government,* First Treatise, §68.

[11]This is the position taken by T.H. Green, *Lectures on the Principles of Political Obligation* (London: Longmans Green, 1931), §50 and John W. Gough, *John Locke's Political Philosophy* (Oxford: Clarendon Press, 1973), pp. 41, 114-15.

[12]John Locke, *Two Treatises of Government,* First Treatise, §§129, 133. See Wolfgang von Leyden, "Introduction" in John Locke, *Essays on the Law of Nature,* Wolfgang von Leyden, ed. (Oxford: Clarendon Press, 1954), p. 20 and Peter Laslett, "Introduction," in Locke, *Two Treatises of Government,* p. 253, footnote 4.

[13]Locke, *Two Treatises of Government,* Second Treatise, §§134, 243.

[14]Ibid., §149.

[15]Ibid., §168.

[16]Ibid., §149.

[17]Ibid., §§134, 243.

[18]Ibid., §240.

[19]Ibid., §149.

[20]Ibid., §139.

[21]Ibid., §149.

[22]Ibid., §240.

[23]See Ernest Barker, "Introduction," in Ernest Barker, ed., *Social Contract* (Oxford: Oxford University Press, 1971), pp. XXI-XXIV and Gough, *John Locke's Political Philosophy,* pp. 143-46.

[24]In the best review of the use of the concept of trust in seventeenth century English political thought, Gough seems to overemphasize the connection between that notion and the idea of popular sovereignty. Nevertheless, he himself refers to writers who used that concept in taking moderate or pro-absolutist

positions. See Gough, *John Locke's Political Philosophy,* pp. 136-71.
   [25]Locke, *Two Treatises of Government,* Second Treatise, §14.
   [26]Ibid., §195.
   [27]For a discussion of Locke's understanding of trust as a moral duty in political practice, see John Dunn, "The concept of 'trust' in the politics of John Locke," in R. Rorty et al., *Philosophy in History* (Cambridge: Cambridge University Press, 1984), pp. 279-300.
   [28]Dunn, "The concept of 'trust'" p. 295.
   [29]See ch. 4, footnote 77.
   [30]Compare Geraint Parry, "Trust, Distrust and Consensus," *British Journal of Political Science,* vol. 6 (1976): 129-42.
   [31]This point is stressed by James Daly, *Sir Robert Filmer and English Political Thought* (Toronto: Toronto University Press, 1979), pp. 47-48.
   [32]Compare Schochet, *Patriarchalism in Political Thought,* p. 140.
   [33]Robert Filmer, "Observations upon Aristotle's Politics," in Robert Filmer, *Patriarcha and Other Political Works of Sir Robert Filmer,* Peter Laslett, ed. (Oxford: Basil Blackwell, 1949), p. 229.
   [34]Filmer, "Patriarcha," p. 62, and "Observations upon Aristotle's Politics," pp. 205-6. Laslett describes this as Filmer's "argument from the relation of authority to will" and relates it to his belief that "only one mind could will effectively and continuously, that there would be no such thing as an agreed or common will, therefore authority must belong as a possession to one individual who wholly can do the willing." See Laslett, "Introduction" in Filmer, *Patiarcha,* p. 18; see also Daly, *Sir Robert Filmer and English Political Thought,* p. 45, footnote 78.
   [35]Daly, *Sir Robert Filmer and English Political Thought,* p. 45.
   [36]Filmer "Observations upon Aristotle's Politics," p. 189.
   [37]Ibid., p. 222.
   [38]Locke, *Two Treatises of Government,* Second Treatise, §§106, 132, 141, 142, 143.
   [39]Ibid., §132. Plamenatz seems to follow this statement of Locke, assuming that the latter does not insist upon putting the legislative power in an elective assembly and, therefore, that for Locke, the form of government is a matter of preference and not of necessity. See John Plamenatz, *Man and Society: Political and Social Theory* (New York: McGraw-Hill, 1963), vol. 1, p. 237. In light of the discussion of the balance of power presented below, this position cannot hold.
   [40]Seliger, who very convincingly discusses Locke's concept of the separation and subordination of powers in terms of balancing authority within civil government, suggests the opposite. See his *Liberal Politics of John Locke,* pp. 328-31. Nevertheless, from the very little that Locke wrote on democracy and aristocracy, it seems impossible to give an account of his concept of suitable constitutional arrangements in these forms of government, which Seliger

The Position and Structure of Civil Government 121

attempts to do. Ibid., pp. 330-331.

[41] Locke, *Two Treatises of Government,* Second Treatise, §107.
[42] Ibid., §143.
[43] Ibid., §91.
[44] Ibid., §151.
[45] Ibid., §152.
[46] Ibid., §152.
[47] Ibid., §152.
[48] Ibid., §138.
[49] Ibid., §138. Also see §§153-7.
[50] Ibid., §§156, 158.
[51] Ibid., §§157-8.
[52] Ibid., §158.
[53] See Laslett's footnote to Locke, *Two Treatises of Government,* Second Treatise, §158.
[54] Gough and Seliger follow Locke's suggestion and treat the executive as the power which undertakes the redistribution of seats. See Gough, *John Locke's Political Philosophy,* p. 111, footnote 3, and Seliger, *Liberal Politics of John Locke,* p. 347.
[55] It is possible to draw this rigorous distinction in Locke's doctrine because he never suggests that the executive, as the power subordinate to the legislature, could act only according to the law of nature. It is only the federative that must act exclusively according to the law of nature, because it operates in the state of nature that prevails among sovereign polities. See Second Treatise, §134; see also §§146-8, 153.
[56] Julian Franklin, *John Locke and the Theory of Sovereignty* (Cambridge: Cambridge University Press, 1978), pp. 53-126; Seliger, *Liberal Politics of John Locke,* pp. 325-327; Ruth W. Grant, *John Locke's Liberalism* (Chicago and London: The University of Chicago Press, 1987), p. 78.
[57] See ch. 4.
[58] This is Ashcraft's position, which I discuss in ch. 6.

Chapter 6

The Concept of Resistance

To reach this point, we have considered the manner in which Filmer and Locke constructed the three elements of their systems. Each thinker presented his first element—paternal power or superhuman agency (H^1) and human or individual agency (C^1), provided them with standards of rationality, then applied these standards to the institution of property. They then proceeded to establish the second element by explaining the relations among individuals (H^2 and C^2), followed by an explanation of the third element, relations between individuals and their government (H^3 and C^3). Filmer argued that these relations were always created and defined by paternal power and reflected its standards of rationality; Locke claimed that they were always created and defined by individual agents and reflected the agents' standards of rationality. In closing my presentation of their models, I shall discuss the consequences of each system: in Filmer, individuals are never in a position to introduce their own standards of rationality into social and political life; in Locke, they are. Moreover, they are always at liberty to reimpose these standards upon the social and political institutions if these institutions fail to act according to them.

To fully understand these consequences, in this chapter I shall present the manner in which the concept of resistance is rejected in Filmer and endorsed in Locke. I shall argue that in Filmer's holistic model resistance is not an issue since he assumes, first, that circumstances which would justify it cannot be found; second, that resistance is not achievable because subjects have no power to oppose their rulers; and third, that engaging in resistance is senseless because it does not change the situation of these subjects. Locke rejects all of these claims. He claims that certain circumstances—such as tyranny, usurpation, and conquest in an unjust war—do justify resistance. Moreover, in a discussion of the state of war between the ruler and his subjects, Locke stresses that resistance is achievable because the subjects use the political power of civil society to oppose the ruler. Finally, since the result of resistance is a profound change in the subjects' situation, Locke claims that it can be a sensible political action.

The question of resistance can be presented in both Filmer and Locke in the purely normative terms of the duty to obey and the right to resist. Filmer's position implies the unconditional prohibition of any resistance, a prohibition that results from giving all rights to the holder of paternal power and all duties to his subjects. In contrast, Locke treats resistance as the right of subjects, which lies at the very core of the normative part of his doctrine. This is a right to oppose any power exercised over civil society which violates the very principles of that society, thus failing to implement its end, the public good. Resistance, then, is the right to restore the principles of civil society and the original position of civil government, which is necessary for civil society's members to fulfill their duties of self-preservation toward God. Hence, it is both a right against any holder of unauthorized might used against civil society, and a duty toward God.

Yet limiting the discussion of resistance to the narrow normative terms of the duty to obey and the right to resist is insufficient to fully understand the role it plays in Filmer's and Locke's models. Instead, the concept of resistance is best understood not by asking whether it is prohibited or permitted but by asking whether either model considers it possible as a rational political action.

To answer this question, three issues must be considered. The first is whether circumstances can be found which would justify resistance; the second, whether resistance is achievable; and the third, whether resistance can in fact remove the reasons for which it was undertaken—in other words, whether engaging in resistance makes sense at all.

Unlike Locke, Filmer does not discuss any of these problems directly. Nevertheless, all three are implicitly addressed in the very structure of his model. The first issue can be traced back to the fundamental premise of his system—that paternal power is the highest terrestrial end.[1] This means that, although the activity of a monarch as the holder of paternal power may be seen in purely voluntarist terms, he is still obliged to follow one duty imposed by God—to preserve paternal power in a form close to that in which Adam exercised it. Accordingly, the monarch is not only a holder of paternal power; he is also its guardian. His tasks as the only lawgiver[2] and only interpreter of law[3] confirm this status. He is also the only authority that is entitled to pass judgment on public affairs in the Filmerian polity. It would be difficult to expect that this Filmerian monarch could find any circumstances justifying resistance; as the guardian of paternal power, he cannot act in any way that would undermine the position of this power—as resistance surely would.

Whether or not one accepts Filmer's unyielding position, the conclusion that there are no circumstances justifying resistance can also be reached even if one assumes that the monarch is not the only one who is entitled to pass judgment on public affairs. Indeed, when Filmer insists that subjects are not allowed to judge whether the commands of their monarch are rightful or not,[4] he underestimates the force of his holistic argument. In the system he created, the holder of paternal power is not the only one who must be its guardian. If Filmer's premises are to be taken seriously—if paternal power is the highest terrestrial end and if it finds its full expression in absolute monarchy—one must conclude that the duty imposed by God (which orders the preservation of a paternal power that resembles that of Genesis) addresses everyone, not just the rulers. Accordingly, all Christian subjects must refrain from passing judgment upon public affairs, if the consequences of such a judgment could undermine the position of that power—as resistance would. For Filmer, then, neither rulers nor ruled can find any circumstances which would justify a right to resist.

The best indication that the holistic model is the only model that leaves no room for conditional obedience can be found in Filmer's efforts to reject any claims to a right to resist that occur under a contractarian model. Indeed, in an effort to make his position against resistance more universal, Filmer sometimes sets aside the principles of his own argument and adopts some elements of the contractarian argument. When he does, he clearly refers to the preservation of mankind (instead of the preservation of paternal power) as the highest terrestrial end, and to judgments on public affairs made by subjects (not by rulers). For example, Filmer rejects Aristotle's definition of tyranny and cautiously states that it is false to assume "that there may be a government only for the benefit of the governors."[5] Later, he goes further; stating the problem straightforwardly, Filmer admits that "the right of fatherly government was ordained by God, for the preservation of mankind" and, accordingly, that "it should be granted, that subjection and protection are reciprocal."[6] However, in his attempt to turn contractarians against the concept of resistance, Filmer's argument becomes practical rather than philosophical. Resistance is now forbidden not because there are no circumstances justifying it but because launching it would threaten the preservation of the people themselves. As Filmer puts it, "if government be hindered, mankind perisheth."[7]

It is difficult to establish whether Filmer believed that adopting some elements of the contractarian argument would be more efficient than using his own holistic argument in persuading his reader that resistance should not be attempted. Nevertheless, the attempt to adapt contractarianism to his doctrine led him astray. The price he paid was the coherence of his own writings, for which he gained nothing in return. Indeed, once Filmer started using some elements of the contractarian argument, he immediately felt forced to admit, in his discussion of obedience in indifferent and non-indifferent things, that subjects had to judge for themselves to what extent they should obey their rulers and that they could find circumstances which made their obedience conditional.[8]

Clearly, Filmer's conclusion that no circumstances justifying resistance can be found was possible only within his holistic model. But what of his thoughts on whether resistance can in fact be achievable? Filmer claims that subjects, even if they find circumstances justifying resistance to their rulers, do not possess the power to resist. Regardless of how sophisticated the political structure of the polity may be, all the power which some of them may exercise is the paternal power of their monarch. This claim results from Filmer's concept of the chain of power, which leads from God through Adam to monarchs, who in turn delegate parts of it to inferior magistrates. Thus, "whatsoever power any people doth lawfully exercise, it must receive it from a supreme power on earth, and practise it with such limitations as that superior power shall appoint."[9] In other words, there is no power which subjects could use against their monarch. As Filmer puts it, "if this supreme power was settled and founded by God himself in the fatherhood, how is it possible for the people to have any right or title to alter or dispose of it otherwise?"[10]

The effectiveness of Filmer's argument against resistance can be tested—on his own terms—by examining how it would operate in two situations: before and after the outbreak of resistance. Before resistance is launched, his argument is very effective indeed. Two of Filmer's earlier moves, which were made to prevent the normative force of his holistic argument from being threatened by empirical facts, assist him here. First, he rejected the distinction between might and right, making it possible for him to treat any use of paternal power as legitimate. Second, he rejected the distinction between the natural and conventional orders, assuming that any political constellation, regardless of how similar or dissimilar it may be to the biblical model, is natural.[11] As a result of Filmer's first move, subjects cannot resist their rulers since they have neither the might nor right to do so; as a result of his second move, since every political constellation embodies political power, his argument stands no matter what kind of government exists. Thus, Filmer can safely claim that resistance is not achievable; in other words, it cannot exist as a political phenomenon.

The same two moves that make Filmer's argument against resistance effective when applied before the outbreak of resistance make his argument completely ineffective after resistance has already taken place. Since in Filmer's view there is no room for a permanent separation between might and right, the might of the subjects who successfully oppose their ruler immediately creates a right on their part. Indeed, though Filmer admits that the right of a lawful king is stronger than that of a usurper, he goes on to point out that "the first usurper hath the best title, being... in possession by the permission of God."[12] Moreover, since any political constellation belongs to the natural order, the post-resistance arrangement is not less legitimate than the pre-resistance one. Accordingly, in Filmer's system there is always room left to justify resistance after the fact.

Although this conclusion is in perfect accordance with his holistic argument, it was not what Filmer wanted his reader to focus on. Still, it would be wrong to assume that his argument slipped away from his control and justified solutions that were unacceptable to him. There is nothing to indicate that Filmer did not agree with the message of his system, which always found the *status quo* justifiable, and which, while ruling out any possibility of resistance *a priori,* legitimized it *a posteriori.* Filmer could not express it more precisely than in his claim: "It skills not which way Kings come by their power, whether by election, donation, succession, or by any other means, for it is still the manner of government by supreme power that makes them properly Kings, and not the means of obtaining their crowns."[13]

However, it would be wrong to think that the Filmerian dialectic presented above, in abbreviated form, encourages resistance. Precisely because of this dialectic, Filmer's answer to the question of whether resistance makes sense must be unequivocally negative. The reason for this lies in the homogeneous character of paternal power, which reflects the unity of might and right. If "all power on earth is either derived or usurped from the fatherly power, there being no other original to be found of any power whatsoever,"[14] then resistance may be undertaken only by using that same power. Accordingly, a successful act of resistance can bring about a change of persons and replace the previous holder of power with a new one, but it is not able to alter the status of that power itself. No resistance can change either the source of the legitimacy of power or the content and extent of the political obligation of its subjects. In other words, no resistance can change the conditions of political obligation, since these conditions are always determined by the same component of human life—paternal power.

In sum, in spite of Filmer's *a posteriori* acceptance of successful resistance, his holistic approach made it possible for him to justify the unconditional obedience of subjects. Filmer assured his reader that resistance cannot be a category of political thought, first, because circumstances which would justify it cannot be found; second, because even if they could be found, resistance would not be achievable; and thirdly, because even if resistance were achievable, it would not change the conditions which had caused it; that is, resistance would not make any sense.

I turn now to Locke's examination of the three propositions regarding the circumstances, possibility, and sensibleness of resistance. With regard to the first of these, the circumstances justifying resistance, Locke replaces Filmer's fundamental premise that paternal power is the highest terrestrial end with the premise that the preservation of the individual and mankind, or *salus populi,* is that end. Moreover, for Locke, the place of the Filmerian monarch, who is the guardian of paternal power, is taken by the people or civil society, who look after their own preservation. This makes it possible for Locke to incorporate into the descriptive part of his doctrine circumstances giving rise to resistance, in the same way that Filmer had been able to deny the existence of such circumstances within the logic of his argument.

Locke presents these circumstances in his chapters on conquest, usurpation, tyranny, and the dissolution of government. In all the cases he discusses, civil society is forced to consider an "Appeal to Heaven," which in his terminology means not prayer but the taking up of arms. The wide range of these different situations would seem to require an analysis to indicate one or more common circumstances justifying resistance. In scholarship, however, the efforts aimed at discovering such circumstances have proven rather unfortunate. Geraint Parry and Richard Ashcraft, two authors who try to present such common circumstances, suggest that it is the tyrannical behavior of rulers which justifies resistance.[15] Given Locke's definition of tyranny as the exercise of power "which no Body can have a Right to,"[16] their interpretation ignores usurpation and conquest, which he defines as "*the Possession of what another has Right to.*"[17] According to this definition, the behavior of the usurper and conqueror cannot be classified *a priori* as tyrannical. Yet both are, in Locke, liable to be resisted unconditionally.[18]

Confining the issue of resistance to the tyrannical behavior of rulers seems to result from a tendency on the part of the interpreters to overemphasize the influence of the historical context in which the *Two Treatises* was written. Indeed, if one presents the circumstances justifying resistance as exclusively referring to the experience of political conflicts in seventeenth century England, it is possible to take the tyrannical behavior of rulers as the only justification of resistance, since at that time Locke ascribed such behavior to the Stuarts. However, it is hard to believe that a purely political approach is in accordance with Locke's treatment of the problem. That Locke took pains to give a long account of usurpation and conquest, two issues which were not of much current political interest for him when he was writing his discourse, clearly indicates that he wanted to present a balanced, comprehensive discussion of the other circumstances that justify resistance in his model.

A more appropriate common feature of all the circumstances which justify legitimate resistance is the use of unauthorized might over civil society. This criterion is wide enough to cover activities undertaken by a tyrant, a usurper, and a conqueror in an unjust war. Moreover, since political power is described by Locke as a right because it is an institutional manifestation of the individual rights of self-preservation,[19] this criterion indicates that the circumstances which justify resistance are to be found in all situations where right is opposed by might[20] on a scale where civil society as a whole is concerned.

When Locke applies the contrast between might and right to this narrower issue, it becomes (in spite of some obvious terminological inconsistencies) a contrast between rebellion and resistance. Rebellion is defined as "an Opposition, not to Persons, but Authority, which is founded only in the Constitutions and Laws of the Government."[21] In other words, rebellion is opposition to political power, which is the only authority in civil society. As Locke puts it, rebels act by virtue of "the pretence they have to Authority, the temptation of force they have in their hands."[22] Resistance is described as a reaction to rebellion;[23] it opposes persons, not authority. To make use of "the Right of resisting" is simply to exercise political power against persons who use "force without Right."[24]

Having stated this general criterion of the circumstances which justify resistance, Locke proceeds to discuss instances from political practice. His interest in making use of a right to resist rulers who have never been entrusted with political power—such as usurpers and conquerors in an unjust war—is purely scholarly and does not go beyond a few biblical references which suit his doctrinal assumptions.[25] The main weight of his discussion is placed upon an examination of various political situations within civil government which might lead to a breach of trust and, consequently, to rebellious activity on the part of some of its members or of the government as a whole.

With obvious reference to the political experience of his own time, Locke scrupulously enumerates circumstances which would justify resistance, pointing to certain of the activities of the executive. He writes of efforts of the executive to replace the will of the legislative with its own, as happens when orders are executed that have no legislative authorization. He deals with the executive's attempts to hinder the legislative from meeting at the proper time, and with its machinations intended to produce a legislative sympathetic to its interests—which it might accomplish, for example, by altering the franchise or electoral districts against the common good, or by bribing and intimidating the electorate or the elected members of Parliament. Locke also considers the executive's efforts to avoid enforcing laws that have been passed by the legislative; and finally, he examines its attempts to subject the legislative and the whole government to foreign domination.[26]

Each of these situations justify the taking up of arms against the government, but only if civil society—or, rather, its majority—decides that the offending activity jeopardizes the very existence of the people as a whole. Locke gives a set of conditions for such a majority decision. According to these, resistance should be undertaken by "the Body of the People" as a whole, civil society ought to judge whether the Cause is "of sufficient moment," whether it is just "to make their Appeal to

Heaven," and lastly, whether they are sure that they have "Right on their side."[27]

Locke's discrimination between might and right is essential to the contractarian explanation of the reasons for resistance (the first issue under discussion). But it also is the point of departure for the second issue, that is, his demonstration of how and why resistance is achievable. By pointing to his distinction, Locke completely rejects Filmer's claim that there is no power which could be used against rulers. To understand this position, one must understand his view of the relation between right and might in the context of the state of war.

Defining this state, Locke writes that "whosoever uses *force without Right*... puts himself into a *state of War* with those, against whom he so uses it."[28] But an incidental use of force does not exclude good faith on the part of the wrongdoer and thus does not automatically bring about a state of war.[29] If an individual is to be treated as an aggressor declaring a state of war, that individual must have a "sedate setled Design" to enslave another.[30] The state of war owes its unique character to a separation of might and right in which the latter is constantly threatened by the former. As such, the state of war is antithetical to the state of nature—both to the state of nature proper, in which might always accompanies right, and to the ordinary state of nature, in which might rarely follows right but never indicates any intention to oppose it. The state of war is similarly antithetical to civil society, where political power is usually exercised in accordance with the public good.

Locke's concept of the state of war—a state which threatens the rights of individuals and civil society alike—applies in a range of contexts. A state of war occurs both when someone uses "force without Right upon a Man's Person" and where there is a use of "Force upon the People without Authority."[31] Accordingly, the emergence of this state is not limited to the context of the state of nature; it can also occur in civil society.[32] The aim of Locke's insistence that a state of war can exist in both these situations is transparent: he wants to make clear that any ruler who deliberately uses force without authority loses, as would any other aggressor, his natural status as a human being and thus gives up the moral link with God and his fellow men, which is his right of self-preservation. Having chosen the status of a beast "with whom Mankind can have neither Society or Security," such a ruler renders himself "liable to be destroied" as a result of successful resistance.[33] This message is of such importance to Locke that he stresses it repeatedly throughout the *Two Treatises with* unprecedented passion and in extremely radical language [34]

Locke's highly emotional treatment of the issue of resistance leads him to neglect the evident theoretical difference between the relation of right to might in different contexts. That is, Locke neglects the possibility that the relation could vary, depending on whether the state of war occurred in the state of nature or in civil society. By taking a step back and looking more closely at the argument, not only can we see how Locke reached this conclusion, we can also notice the theoretical difference that he does not point out. The background to do this can be found in his discussion of might and right in civil society.

The might which is at the disposal of the aggressor who attacks an innocent in the state of nature—and turns it into the state of war—is merely the aggressor's physical capacity to use force. This is based upon no right and thus lacks any normative status or moral character. It therefore remains confined to the descriptive part of Locke's doctrine. In the state of nature, or, more specifically, in its ordinary variety, the aggressor's might faces two obstacles. Not only does he face the innocent's right (the natural right of self-preservation), but also the innocent's might, which is embodied in the two natural powers —especially the second natural power, to punish crimes committed against the law of nature. While it is true that the innocent's might opposes the aggressor's in the factual sphere (because, like the might of the aggressor, it is a physical capacity to use force), its link to the right it defends gives it the normative status and moral character of a right, placing it in the normative part of Locke's doctrine. The relation between the two types of might described here is identical to the relation between civil society and the usurper or conqueror: Civil society resists the might of the usurper or conqueror using its own might—in this case political power rather than the two natural powers. But as with the case just discussed, the state of war between the two occurs in the state of nature, because civil society has never entrusted either the usurper or the conqueror with political power.

The relation between the two types of might is essentially different if the state of war exists between civil society and a ruler of that society who has previously been entrusted with political power. Having entrusted the ruler with this power, civil society retains its right to preserve mankind but does not have any might at its disposal—that is, it lacks the physical capacity for using force. This capacity is entirely at the disposal of the ruler who is the head of civil government. Provided the ruler's might defends civil society's right, the might shares the normative status and moral character of the right and its place in the normative part of Locke's doctrine. However, as soon as the ruler declares his intention to use force without right against his subjects, the unity of right and might ceases. The only might which can be used by the ruler from that point on is that which he exercises as a private individual.[35] Political power, regardless of who controls it at a given moment, can never be used against civil society, just as the two natural powers in the state of nature cannot be used against an innocent individual either by himself or by anybody else. Therefore, political power, which never loses its normative status and moral character, automatically reverts to civil society in order to defend that society.[36] This reversion introduces all the attributes of the state of war into the polity. Civil society's right of preservation is defended by its might—its political power—against the unauthorized might of its former ruler.

Clearly, then, according to Locke's model of social relations resistance is achievable. But to understand its place within that model it is advisable to consider the effects of successful resistance upon various parties under his system.

For Filmer resistance was not an issue; it did not make any sense, because the only change it could bring about was a change of the particular people who exercised paternal power. For Locke, such a change is a visible sign of successful resistance, but this does not fully account for the effects of such resistance, since a change of ruler is not its original aim. Indeed, regardless of whether the monarch is personally responsible for the decisions of his inferior officers, he dethrones himself whenever he puts himself in a state of war with his subjects.[37] Accordingly, he will be punished as any other aggressor in this state. Nevertheless, for Locke the fundamental objective of resistance is not the punishment of the former ruler (though this is stressed throughout the *Second Treatise*); rather, it is the fulfillment of the will of the people to "put the rule into such hands, which may secure to them the ends for which Government was at first errected."[38] This end cannot be achieved by a mere change of persons; it requires a change of the power which they exercise. The effect of resistance is to replace unauthorized might used over civil society with legitimate political power.

This means that the result of successful resistance concerns not only the monarch, as in Filmer's doctrine, but the very condition of civil society as a whole and of every human being in it. Locke stresses this point when he compares the state of affairs before and after successful resistance. The state of affairs before successful resistance, when the use of unauthorized might still prevails, is presented as the ruler's efforts "*to take away, and destroy the Property of the People*, or to reduce them to Slavery."[39] The state of affairs after successful resistance, when legitimate political power operates, is described as the fulfillment of "the end why People entered into Society," which is "to be preserved one intire, free, independent Society, to be governed by its own Laws."[40] This change of power implies a profound alteration in the character of the ruler's legitimacy and the subjects' obligations. Successful resistance brings an end to both the *de facto* legitimacy of the holders of unauthorized might, who have at their disposal the physical capacity to enforce obedience, and the natural obligations of the subjects, who are obliged to obey in order to avoid a threat to their preservation.[41] The holders of unauthorized might are replaced by politically legitimate rulers, who derive their authority from the consent of their subjects. This consent, in turn, creates political obligations on the subjects' part. What follows from this analysis is that successful resistance does indeed remove the reasons for which it was undertaken. Contrary to the position represented by Filmer, therefore, resistance in Locke makes sense; it is a rational political action. It restores the principles of civil society and the original position of civil government as they were set up in the acts of social contract and political trusteeship.

The three points just examined—that there are situations in which subjects have good reasons to take up arms against their rulers; that subjects have not only the right but also the necessary might to do this; and that such action may be profoundly sensible—are central to Locke's pro-resistance stance in the *Second Treatise*. It is now possible to indicate the place and function of resistance in the structure of his argument.

For Locke, resistance is the guarantee that the normative part of his doctrine is not merely declarative, but also applicable to political practice. Without the right of resistance, neither the individual in civil society nor civil society itself could observe the provisions of the law of nature; they would be unable to preserve their very being. Resistance is, therefore, the guarantee that the conventional order, as it was established by men in the act of social contract, can work in accordance with the moral principles of the natural order created by God.

This conclusion stands in disagreement with Richard Ashcraft's interpretation, which is the most elaborate analysis of Locke's concept of resistance to date. Since it is incompatible with some crucial elements of the contractarian model presented here, it is worth more detailed critical evaluation.

Ashcraft rests his interpretation upon three claims.[42] The first is that, as Locke suggests at one point,[43] the dissolution of government causes the members of civil society to return to the state of nature. Locke, claims Ashcraft, invariably runs together the establishment of civil society with the setting up of the legislative;[44] therefore, until the legislative is established, with a specific form of government giving it shape, the people remain in the state of nature.[45] Resistance is thus launched not by civil society, which is formed along with the government, but rather by individuals in the state of nature. But in order to carry out such resistance, it is, as Locke states, necessary for them to "act as one body."[46] Ashcraft therefore assumes that these individuals are bound together by extrapolitical ties which are expressed, as he puts it, in "the organized act of revolution." Ashcraft's second claim is that both the state of nature and the state of war have a profoundly egalitarian character, since there, as Locke writes, "there is no superiority or jurisdiction" among men. His third, crucial claim refers to Locke's vigorous insistence, against the position represented by Barclay, that the king as a party in the state of war should be treated as any other person without "due reverence and respect," that is, he should be deprived both of his life and estate.

The strongest support for Ashcraft's first claim is to be found in a passage where Locke writes that an individual who joins civil society "can never be again in the liberty of the state of Nature; unless by any Calamity, the Government he was under, comes to be dissolved."[47] Unfortunately, Ashcraft does not consider this in the context of Locke's clear distinction between the dissolution of government and the dissolution of society. This distinction indicates that governments can be dissolved from within as an effect of resistance, as well as from without as a result of conquest. The latter dissolves society itself and, in so doing, destroys government, since "where the Society is dissolved, the Government cannot remain."[48] In the light of this distinction, it is valid to interpret the passage concerning the return to the state of nature as being in accordance with the rest of Locke's statements on resistance, rather than, as Ashcraft reads it, in contradiction to them. "[A]ny Calamity" should then be taken to mean a conquest which causes the dissolution of society and government. Further textual support for Ashcraft's first claim is even less convincing. Contrary to Ashcraft's insistence, Locke clearly states that civil society can survive as a political body without the legislative, since after the dissolution of government from within, political power "reverts to the Society, and the People have a Right to act as Supreme, and continue the Legislative in themselves."[49] Moreover, Ashcraft's claim that resistance is carried out by individuals who are united in the state of nature by "the organized act of revolution" finds no textual support in the *Second Treatise*; indeed, it contradicts the letter and logic of Locke's account of resistance. In Locke such resistance cannot take place without the support of the majority,[50] which emerges exclusively in civil society and not in the state of nature. With no support in Locke for Ashcraft's "organized act of revolution," one must conclude that his claim offers a construct of his own making, rather than one of Locke's.

The egalitarianism of the state of nature and state of war, which Ashcraft attributes to Locke in his second claim, is circumscribed; in the case of the state of nature, as has been presented above, it is clearly limited to the moral status enjoyed by all human beings;[51] in the state of war, it is limited by the fact that aggressors lack any human status.

Therefore, Ashcraft's third claim, that resistance is aimed against "the social and political status" of the king, and, in addition to him, of "other individuals as property-owners or members of the aristocracy," is again in disagreement with the letter and structure of Locke's presentation of the issue. Locke clearly indicates that in the state of war the efforts of the innocent party should be aimed against the person of the aggressor and not his social position: the aggressor's estate ought to be saved if its confiscation might threaten the preservation of others, especially the families of the aggressors who are not responsible for their wrongdoing.[52] Accordingly, resistance does not deprive any group of "individuals as property-owners or members of the aristocracy" of their social status—as Ashcraft believes—but only those among this group who abused the political power with which they had been entrusted. In fact, discussions of "social status" and of destroying a "class" of people is not even incidentally in Locke's philosophical vocabulary, let alone an integral part of his own doctrine.

In light of the textual evidence of the *Second Treatise*, the credibility of Ashcraft's interpretative efforts is clearly disputable. Equally disputable is the result of his efforts: the presentation of Locke's concept of resistance as a notion of social revolution. Scholarly suggestions of this kind had been made before Ashcraft presented his interpretation. Indeed, the closest one to Ashcraft's claimed that Lockean principles were not implemented until the Bolshevik revolution.[53] There is no need to offer a detailed challenge to specific interpretations here. It is, however, important to indicate that there is no room for social revolution within Locke's contractarian model.

To prove this, it is enough to compare Ashcraft's concept of social revolution in Locke, which emerges from his reading of the *Second Treatise*, with the account of resistance stated by Locke himself and discussed above. The result of social *revolution* is the dissolution of civil society as a political unity, that is, the destruction of the conventional order. The effect of *resistance*, as Locke defines it, is the preservation of that order. Revolution is a means used by individuals who are outside civil society, in the state of nature; resistance is a means at the disposal of civil society itself. According to the concept of revolution, civil society is an object which, after its dissolution as a political unity, undergoes a structural transformation achieved from outside, that is, from the state of nature. According to the concept of resistance, civil society is a subject which acts by itself to change its political surroundings.

This is not to say that it is impossible to argue in Ashcraft's favor that, despite the lack of textual support for it in the *Second Treatise,* the concept of social revolution is still reconcilable with the contractarian model itself. That is, it is possible to argue that, contrary to the impression given above, revolution does not undermine the status of civil society as a subject. Indeed, one could argue that revolution is not an anonymous force operating from outside civil society, but rather that it is an expression of the will of the majority of society's members. The latter, as the creators of civil society, can dissolve it and then, after transforming its social structure in the state of nature, reestablish it in the act of a new social contract.

The point is, though, that this is not Locke's position. Locke does not discuss or even mention the dissolution of society from within. This is not because there is a lack of historical precedent for the kind of revolution just described; after all, Locke did not hesitate to include the hypothesis of a state of nature proper in his doctrine, even though (as shown above) the historicity of such a state is doubtful.[54] In fact, the idea of a revolution which could dissolve and then reestablish civil society would have suited Locke's highly rationalistic, individualistic doctrine. There must be some reason why he did not incorporate such an idea, apart from its lack of historical precedent. It seems likely that his silence on this matter results from the fact that, given the premises of the normative part of Locke's doctrine, the dissolution of civil society from within would have been completely pointless. Locke emphasizes many times that civil society can always choose a form of government as it pleases;[55] but he never says that individuals in the state of nature are in a position to choose the form of civil society that they would like to set up. The form of civil society, or, more precisely, its principles, are beyond human choice. They are granted. They conform to the provisions of the law of nature, since they are constructed so that civil society's members may follow this law. Therefore, there can be only one unchangeable form of civil society.[56] If the members of civil society had decided to dissolve it in order to carry out their revolutionary action, as Ashcraft believes, they would have had to have set up precisely the same society again afterwards. The only alternative to civil society which Locke leaves in the normative part of his doctrine is not another form of civil society but the state of nature. The essence of the status of civil society as a subject in Locke's contractarian model is expressed by the fact that it exists as it is or not at all. The concept of resistance confirms this status; the notion of social revolution rules it out.

Summary

In this chapter, I presented the positions of Filmer and Locke on resistance. Filmer argues that resistance is unjustified, impossible to carry out, and, finally, pointless as a political action. Locke claims that resistance is justified in some cases, possible to carry out, and reasonable as a political action.

In scholarship, Locke's position on resistance is rarely considered in the context of his polemic with Filmer. But even when scholars discuss it in this context they usually limit their discussion—as, for example, John Dunn does[57]—to the general observation that Filmer found resistance absolutely unjustified while Locke justified it in a whole spectrum of circumstances. What is missing in these observations is the realization that the whole body of Locke's discussion of resistance is an integral part of his dispute with Filmer. Indeed, as I hope to have illustrated, Locke's presentation of the operation of such concepts as consent, political power, political legitimacy, and political obligation in the extreme political conditions of resistance resulted from his need to reject the position of his opponent and present a comprehensive alternative to it.

---

[1]See ch. 5.
[2]Robert Filmer, "Patriarcha," in Robert Filmer, *Patriarcha and Other Political Works of Sir Robert Filmer*, Peter Laslett, ed. (Oxford: Basil

Blackwell, 1949), pp. 106-08, 119-20.
  ³Ibid., pp. 106-13.
  ⁴Ibid., pp. 93-94.
  ⁵Robert Filmer, "Observations upon Aristotle's Politics," in Robert Filmer, *Patriarcha and Other Political Works of Sir Robert Filmer,* Peter Laslett, ed. (Oxford: Basil Blackwell, 1949), p. 204.
  ⁶Robert Filmer, "Directions for Obedience to Government in Dangerous or Doubtful Times," in Robert Filmer, *Patriarcha and Other Political Works of Sir Robert Filmer,* Peter Laslett, ed. (Oxford: Basil Blackwell, 1949), p. 234.
  ⁷Ibid., p. 233.
  ⁸Ibid., pp. 234-35.
  ⁹Robert Filmer, "Anarchy of a Limited or Mixed Monarchy," in Robert Filmer, *Patriarcha and Other Political Works of Sir Robert Filmer,* Peter Laslett, ed. (Oxford: Basil Blackwell, 1949), p. 290.
  ¹⁰Filmer, "Directions for Obedience to Government," p. 283.
  ¹¹See ch. 2.
  ¹²Filmer, "Directions for Obedience to Government," p. 232.
  ¹³Filmer, "Patriarcha," p. 106. The conviction that Filmer treats paternal power as its own justification is shared by W. H. Greenleaf, *Order, Empiricism and Politics: Two Traditions of English Political Thought 1500-1700* (Westport, Connecticut: Greenwood Press, 1980), p. 86; John Plamenatz, *Man and Society: Political and Social Theory* (New York: McGraw-Hill, 1963), p. 184, and James Daly, *Sir Robert Filmer and English Political Thought* (Toronto: Toronto University Press, 1978), p. 106.
  ¹⁴Filmer, "Directions for Obedience to Government," p. 233.
  ¹⁵See Geraint Parry, *John Locke* (London: George Allen & Unwin, 1978), p. 136 and Richard Ashcraft, *Locke's Two Treatises of Government* (London: Allen & Unwin, 1987), pp. 196-228.
  ¹⁶John Locke, *Two Treatises of Government,* Peter Laslett, ed. (Cambridge: Cambridge University Press, 1988), Second Treatise, §199.
  ¹⁷Ibid., §197.
  ¹⁸Ibid., §§176, 196, 26. This is a position taken by Ashcraft in his *Locke's Two Treatises of Government,* pp. 212-15.
  ¹⁹See ch. 4, sec. I and III.
  ²⁰In light of this criterion, the account of the Lockean concept of resistance as that which is aimed against despotical power is profoundly misleading. It is presented as such, for instance, in M. Susan Power, "John Locke: Revolution, Resistance, or Opposition?" *Interpretation,* vol. 9, No. 2 & 3 (1981), p. 231, and Ashcraft, *Locke's Two Treatises of Government,* p. 211. Contrary to Ashcraft's claim, despotical power in Locke has nothing in common with tyranny, since a holder of that power, unlike a tyrant, has a right on his side. His might is based upon "the right of war, a liberty to kill the aggressor," which reaches back to the right of self-preservation of the innocent (Second Treatise, §169). This Locke

simply calls "a Despotical Right" (ibid., §196). As such, despotical power is exercised exclusively over "Captives, taken in a just and lawful War"—that is, people "who are stripp'd of all property," and thus of all rights (ibid., §173).

[21] Locke, *Two Treatises of Government,* Second Treatise, §226.

[22] Ibid., §226.

[23] Ibid., §§230-32.

[24] In spite of the fundamental significance of the distinction between resistance and rebellion in his argument, Locke is sometimes hopelessly careless about maintaining a clear distinction in the text. Accordingly, rebellion is at some places used as a synonym for resistance (Locke, *Two Treatises of Government,* Second Treatise, §§196, 224, 227, 228). Yet the carelessness of some scholars who comment on Locke's account of resistance is even greater and much more confusing than that of Locke himself; they completely overlook Locke's distinction between resistance and rebellion in the text of the Second Treatise and always use these terms interchangeably. Consequently, they introduce rebellion into the normative part of Locke's doctrine and discuss "the right of rebellion" or "a right to rebellion" which, careless as he was, Locke never discussed. See Wolfgang von Leyden, *Hobbes and Locke* (New York: St. Martin's Press, 1982), p. 186, and Power, "John Locke: Revolution, Resistance, or Opposition," pp. 231-40, especially 234. This failure is still less understandable since it has been noted in scholarship that Locke clearly used both terms in accordance with their meanings within two traditions of political thought: that of Thomism in the case of rebellion, where it is treated as an act of a tyrannical prince (Martin Seliger, *Liberal Politics of John Locke* [New York: Praeger, 1968], p. 316), and that of Calvinism in the case of resistance, where it is regarded as a duty and a right (John Dunn, *The Political Thought of John Locke* [Cambridge: Cambridge University Press, 1969], pp. 182- 83). For a discussion of resistance understood as a duty or a right in sixteenth century Calvinist theories, see Quentin Skinner, *The Foundations of Modern Political Thought* (Cambridge: Cambridge University Press, 1978), vol. II.

[25] Locke, *Two Treatises of Government,* Second Treatise, §196.

[26] Ibid., §§214-19, 222.

[27] Ibid., §168. See also §§242-43, 176.

[28] Ibid., §232.

[29] Ibid., §20.

[30] Ibid., §16; compare §20.

[31] Ibid., §§19, 155.

[32] Ibid., §17.

[33] Ibid., §§11, 172.

[34] For two different accounts of Locke's radical language in his discussion of the state of war, see Dunn, *Political Thought of John Locke,* pp. 165-71, and Richard Ashcraft, *Radical Politics and Locke's Two Treatises of Government* (Princeton: Princeton University Press, 1986), pp. 338-405.

The Concept of Resistance 141

[35] Locke, *Two Treatises of Government,* Second Treatise, §237.
[36] Ibid., §243.
[37] Ibid., §§205, 239.
[38] Ibid., §225.
[39] Ibid., §222.
[40] Ibid., §217.
[41] See ch. 4, sec. III.
[42] Ashcraft, *Locke's Two Treatises of Government,* pp. 216-28.
[43] Locke, *Two Treatises of Government,* Second Treatise, §121.
[44] Ibid., §§87, 89.
[45] Ibid., §132.
[46] Ibid., §211.
[47] Ibid., §121.
[48] Ibid., §211. Also see § 212.
[49] Ibid., §243. For a slightly different interpretation, see Nathan Tarcov, "Locke's Second Treatise and 'The Best Fence Against Rebellion'," *Review of Politics,* vol. 43 (1981) and Ruth W. Grant, *John Locke's Liberalism* (Chicago and London: University of Chicago Press, 1987), pp. 148-55. They distinguish between the alteration of the legislative (Locke, *Two Treatises of Government,* Second Treatise, § 212-20) and breach of trust (Locke, *Two Treatises of Government,* Second Treatise § 221- 22); the first dissolves society, the second does not. But even this interpretation cannot support Ashcraft's position, since both these authors assume that the dissolution of society rules out resistance.
[50] Locke, *Two Treatises of Government,* Second Treatise, §209, compare §§97-99.
[51] Ibid., §54 and ch. 2 above.
[52] Ibid., §§180-184.
[53] G.A. Zaichenko, *Locke* (Moskva: Izdatelstvo Mysl, 1973), pp. 170-171.
[54] See ch. 2, footnote 34.
[55] Locke, *Two Treatises of Government,* Second Treatise, §§106, 132, 141, 142, 143.
[56] This remark refers only to individuals in the state of nature in general. This does not mean, of course, that particular individuals in the state of nature—or indeed, as was indicated in Locke's discussion of emigration in civil society (presented earlier in ch. 4, sec. IV)—cannot join the particular civil society they choose. The point is that the normative status of all the civil societies chosen by particular individuals is the same.
[57] Dunn, *Political Thought of John Locke,* p. 177.

Conclusion

The main point I have pressed upon the reader throughout this book is that, when considered from the perspective of his controversy with Robert Filmer, John Locke emerges as a contractarian thinker whose doctrine has a broad conceptual dimension that remains significant for contemporary political theory. However, just as Filmer and Locke did not wish to limit the influence of their works only to the scholarly disputes of their own time, so the present relevance of their clash cannot be limited to the routine, ongoing debate between liberals and communitarians—the modern followers of the contractarian and holistic traditions in academia.

Filmer and Locke constructed their holistic and contractarian models in full agreement with their best understanding of sociopolitical processes. They believed in the explanatory value of their models as well as in their political usefulness; each thinker meant his model to serve as a remedy against the political conflicts tearing apart his country.[1] It is even likely that each would be eager to live in the system he devised. Yet the majority of Englishmen did not share this enthusiasm: they neither believed in the explanatory value of the models nor did they see them as blueprints for a well-ordered society. Seventeenth century England neither became as absolutist as the polity that emerges from *Patriarcha* nor as rationalist and individualist as that offered in the *Two Treatises*.

Interestingly enough, both models have acquired new currency and have had their explanatory value affirmed in more recent times. Indeed, as Sir Karl Popper reminds us, the spectacular development of nineteenth century holistic thought, especially in the doctrines of Hegel and Marx, bore fruit in the emergence of twentieth century "closed societies."[2] Moreover, experience with consensual government culminated in the practice of twentieth century "open societies."

In political practice, the twentieth century holist, i.e., a supporter of the Marxist, nationalist, or religious state, despite his different philosophical perspective and political experience, would find himself in basic agreement with Filmer's holism regarding his vision of the relations between individuals, society, and the state. Like Filmer, he refers to metaphysical agents such as productive forces, the nation, or God as driving sociopolitical processes. He believes in the priority of the social whole, that is, of the class, nation, or religious community, over the individual. He ascribes a natural character to the sociopolitical structure, conforms the individual to society and society to the state, and finds resistance to government in that state illegitimate. Similarly, an advocate of the twentieth century liberal state would agree with most of Locke's contractarianism. Like Locke, he sees sociopolitical processes as phenomena created by human agents. He bases the sociopolitical system on the rights, interests, and needs of these agents. Finally, he considers the relations between individuals, society, and the state man-made, he argues for government's dependency on society, and he justifies resistance in politically extreme situations.

Furthermore, like Filmer, who flatly dismissed contractarianism as nothing more than anarchy,[3] and Locke, who quickly condemned holism as slavery,[4] contemporary holists and contractarians in the world of political practice have basic problems understanding the emergence, the inner order, and the performance of the sociopolitical systems they reject. Using a critical apparatus shaped by their own perspectives, they believe that the only rational form in which humans can live together is in the systems they support; opposing systems are a gigantic violation of that rationality.

The best contemporary example of the incompatibility of the holistic and contractarian visions can be found in their different perceptions of the twentieth century Marxist state, the most powerful application of a holistic model in political practice. A supporter of such a state evaluates its emergence in positive, holistic terms: he points to the historically inevitable outcome of the class struggle that led to the establishment of new patterns of class domination. Accordingly, he sees the recent demise of the Marxist state in Europe in negative, equally holistic terms: he claims that reactionary activities of class enemies led to a breakdown of the sociopolitical unity of the working class and gave way to a counterrevolutionary takeover attempting to turn back the wheel of history.[5] A liberal opponent of the Marxist state would present the same phenomena in a very different way. He stresses, in true contractarian fashion, its negative agenda: the violations of individual rights, the subversion of civil society, and the overthrow of civil government. Thus, he positively evaluates its collapse by finding dissident activities constructive, the creation of pockets of civil society desirable, and the defeat of oppressive governments necessary.[6]

Attempts to base sociopolitical systems on holistic models did not disappear with the latest collapse of most Marxist states; nationalist and religious polities are still considered intellectually and politically attractive alternatives to their liberal counterpart. Thus, as long as liberally minded man does not stand alone, victorious on history's playground,[7] Locke's controversy with Filmer will maintain its philosophical and political relevance.

---

[1] See ch. 1, footnotes 14, 15.
[2] Karl Popper, *The Open Society and Its Enemies* (London: G. Routledge and Sons, 1945).
[3] Robert Filmer, "The Anarchy of a Limited or Mixed Monarchy," in Robert Filmer, *Patriarcha and Other Political Works of Sir Robert Filmer,* Peter Laslett, ed. (Oxford: Basil Blackwell, 1949).
[4] John Locke, *Two Treatises of Government,* Peter Laslett, ed. (Cambridge: Cambridge University Press, 1988), First Treatise, §§1-4.
[5] For the inadequacy of Marxist analysis of the processes leading to the collapse of the Soviet-type system, see Andrew Arato, *From Neo-Marxism to Democratic Theory: Essays on the Critical Theory of Soviet-Type Societies* (M.E. Sharpe: Armonk, New York, 1993).
[6] For a contractarian interpretation of the collapse of Marxist state, see my "Some Thoughts on Civil Society in Eastern Europe and the Lockean Contractarian Approach," *Political Studies,* XXXV, (1987): 573-592 and "The State of Enslavement: the East European Substitute for the State of Nature," *Political Studies,* XXXIX, (1991): 253-269. Compare also my "Introduction" in *The Reemergence of Civil Society in Eastern Europe and the Soviet Union,* Zbigniew Rau, ed. (Boulder: Westview Press, 1991), pp. 1-24.
[7] For such a greatly oversimplified vision, see Francis Fukuyama, *The End of History and the Last Man* (New York: Free Press, 1992).

INDEX

Absolute Spirit, 15

absolutism, 6, 34, 69, 75-76, 78, 94, 116; and prerogative, 79-80; the only form of government in Filmer, 115, 125-126

Adam, 26, 28, 43-45, 106, 115

Aglim, John, 40n

Aquinas, 16, 58-60n

Arato, Andrew, 145n

Aristotle, 21n, 120n

Ashcraft, Richard, 1, 4n, 22n, 35, 36n, 40-41n, 65n, 94, 121n, 129, 134-138, 139-141n

Atwood, William, 23n

Axtell, James L., 64n

Bible, 26

Barbeyrac, Jean, 61n

Barker, Sir Ernest, 20, 23n, 112-113, 119n

Barz, William G., 39n

Baxter, Richard, 61n

Berlin, Isaiah, 97n

Bodin, Jean, 21n, 109

Bradley, F.H., 22n

Braverman, Henry, 63n

causality, 11

charity, 45, 49, 52, 57

Charles I, 114

Cherno, Melvin, 64n

children, 6, 7, 26, 32, 44, 67

civil government, 2, 6, 10, 30, 34, 69, 82, 87, 90, 92-94, 105-106, 123-124, 126-127, 129-130, 133-134, 136-137, 144-145; distinquished from civil society, 69; relations with civil society, 107-109; and sovereignty, 109-112; and trust, 112-114; structure of, 115-118; balance of powers, 116; separation of legislative from executive, 115; dissolution of, 128, 135-136

civil society, 2-3, 10, 28, 34, 43-44, 51-52, 54-55, 67-69, 74, 82, 129, 145; definition of, 69; principles of, 70; property in, 44, 53-56; voluntary character of, 68, 82, 90-93; as remedy against the state of nature, 72; political power created in, 72; and limits of political power, 74-80; royal prerogative in, 78-80; membership by consent, 82-89; political legitimacy in, 82-89; entrance in, 90-92; emigration from, 92-93; relations between might and right in, 132; its relations with civil government, 107-109; and the structure of civil government, 115-118; and sovereignty, 109-112; and trust, 112-114; and resistance, 124, 129-133, 135-138

Clark, J.C.D., 6, 20n

Colleti, Lucio, 23n

Colman, John, 37n

common good, 10, 45, 54, 107, 108, 110, 111, 113, 115, 124, 130-131

communitarianism, 3, 143

conquest, 28, 32, 124, 128-130, 132, 136

consent, 2, 51, 56, 68, 70, 75, 134, 138; and property, 48-49; money introduced by, 54; as foundation of civil society, 73; as criterion of political legitimacy, 80-89; as basis of political obligation, 82-84; tacit and express, 85-87; and voluntary character of civil society, 90-93

contractarianism, 2, 3, 5, 7

contractarian model, 13-19, 25, 44, 67, 75, 79, 83, 89-90, 92-93, 105, 115, 124-125, 134, 136-138, 143

contractarian tradition, 14-19

Cox, Richard, 35, 41n, 98n

Cranston, Maurice, 62n

Crespy, Joseph, 41n, 98n

Cress, Donald A., 22n

Cromwell, Oliver, 115

Church of England, 6

Daly, James, 8, 21n, 58n, 120n, 139n

de Beer, E.S., 94n

den Hartogh, Govert, 65n

Digges, Dully, 23n

distributive justice, 55

divine law, 6, 15, 26, 49

Dunn, John, 1, 4n, 35, 35n, 37-38n, 41n, 62n, 64-65n, 82, 94, 100-103n, 120n, 138, 140-141n

England, 6, 143, 7, 52, 85, 129, 143

Euchner, Walter, 61n

family, 6, 8, 26, 34, 44, 49-50, 92, 136

Farrell, Daniel, 120n

fathers, 6, 7, 26, 44, 68, 80, 106, 126, 128

Ferguson, Robert, 23n

Fox, Burne H.R., 62n

Franklin, Julian, 118, 121n

freedom, 31, 68, 90, 91; as license in Filmer, 77; as subjection to law in Locke, 77; negative and positive, 78

Fukuyama, Francis, 145n

Gay, Peter, 22n

Gierke, Otto, 20

Gilby, T., 58n

Glenn, Gary, 96-97n

God, 15, 26-29, 33, 45, 47, 50, 54, 68-69, 73-75, 78, 80-81. 82, 84, 90, 93, 106-108, 110-111, 113, 124-127, 131, 134, 144

Golden rule, 28

Index 149

Goldwin, Robert, 35, 41n, 98n

Gough, J.W., 20, 23n, 100n, 112-113, 119-121n

Government, *see* civil government

Grant, Ruth, 65n, 94, 103n, 118, 121n, 141n,

Gray, John, 98n

Greek Christians, 30

Green, T.H., 119n

Greenleaf, W.H., 8, 9, 21n, 139n

Grotius, 21n, 26, 47, 59n, 66n, 102n

Hampton, Jean, 18, 23n

Hayek, F.A., 22n

Hegel, 15, 19, 144

Hinton R.W.K., 7, 20n

Hobbes, 6, 7, 8, 13, 15, 17, 18, 21-22n, 27, 28, 29, 36n, 61n, 85, 101n

holism, 2, 3, 5, 10; as alternative to methodological individualism, 11

holistic model, 11-19, 25, 44-45, 69-70, 124-126, 143-145

holistic tradition, 14-19

Hunton, Philip, 19, 21n, 23n

individualism, 2; methodological, 5, 11-13

individualistic model, 5, 11-13

inheritance, 45, 49, 57

James, Duke of York, 21n

James, Susan, 22n

Johnson, Merwyn S., 37n, 39n

Kant, 15, 17-18

Kendall, Wilmoore, 39n, 98n, 102n

Kennet, Basil, 61n

King, Lord Peter, 38n, 58n

kings, 26-27, 44, 69, 71-72, 76-77, 88, 127, 135-136

Krieger, Leonard, 38n

labor, 45, 47, 49-53, 55, 57; alienation of, 50-52

Laslett, Peter, 1, 4n, 5, 6, 20-22n, 36-37n, 39n, 57-59n, 61-63n, 65n, 100n, 118-121n, 138-139n, 145n

liberalism, liberal, 3, 143-145

Mack, Eric, 65n

Mackenzie, George Sir, 58n

Macpherson, C.B., 51, 52, 56, 57, 58n, 61n, 63-64n, 98n, 101n

macroscopic laws, 9

Magoffin, Ralf van Deman, 59n

majority rule, 68, 100, 115, 130, 136-137; rejected by Filmer, 87-88; in Locke, 72, 88-89, 93

Mandelbaum, M., 22n

Marxism, 3, 15, 50, 144-145; and the interpretation of property in Locke, 50-53

Maxwell, John, 23n

Medick, Hans, 38n, 41n

Mellor, D.H., 22n

Milton, John, 21n, 36n, 97n

money, 51, 53, 54, 82

nationalism, 3, 144-145

natural justice, 50, 55

natural law, 45-48, 53-55, 57, 71, 78, 80, 85, 87-88, 107, 111, 113, 118; in Filmer, 26-27; in Locke, 28, 31, 34-35, 71, 74, 77, 87-88; and royal prerogative, 79-80

natural political authority, 91, 92; in Filmer, 80-81, 89; absent in Locke, 82, 84, 88, 89, 90, 91, 92

natural political duty, in Filmer, 68; in Locke, 68

natural power, 29-30, 55-56, 107-109, 132-133; as source of political power, 71-73; and the limits of political power, 74; and royal prerogative, 79-80; and consent, 83

natural rights, 55; and property, 48, 51, 54; to the means of preservation, 48, 51; of preservation, 71, 81, 132-133; and the prohibition of suicide, 75; and emigration, 92

Niddhitch, Peter H., 37n, 96n

Nozick, Robert, 102n

Oldfather C.H. & W.A., 38n

Olivecrona, Karl, 60-61n, 64

O'Neill, J., 22n

Parry, Geraint, 40n, 101n, 120n, 129, 139n

paternal power, 9, 15, 25, 44, 105-107, 114-115, 118; its theological origin, 26; and right and might, 26-28; and right and wrong, 26-28; and the unity of power and property, 45, 50, 57; subjection to as natural status of man, 68, 70, 94; unlimited, 73, 76; as natural political authority, 80; and the absence of resistance, 123-125, 128, 133

patriarchalism, 2, 19; the essence of, 6-8; as alternative to Locke's system, 7; as alternative to contractarianism, 7

Paul, Ellen Frankel, 65n

Pelczynski, Zbigniew, 98n

Pitkin, Hanna, 82, 100n

Plamenatz, John, 82, 100n, 120n, 139n

Polin, Raymond, 97n

political legitimacy, 68, 70, 94, 138; unconditional in Filmer, 69, 80, 81, 94; conditional in Locke, 69, 94; and political obligation, 81; and tyranny and usurpation, 82-84

political obligation, 3, 68, 70, 84, 86, 128, 134, 138; unconditional in Filmer, 68-69, 80, 81, 94; conditional in Locke, 69, 81-82; based on consent, 82-84, 86, 94

polis, 15

Popper, Karl Sir, 20, 22n, 145n

positive laws, 26, 27, 77, 79, 87, 118

power, 6, 29, 30, 68, 70-72, 75, 88, 124, 126; absolute, arbitrary, 59, 75, 79, 80; despotical, 30; economic, 44; executive, 56, 68, 73, 108, 116-118, 138; federative, 69; legislative, 56, 68, 73, 108, 110-112, 116-118, 130, 135-136; political, 30, 34, 67-70, 107-109, 124, 129-135; sovereign, 8-9; *see also* Marxism; natural power; paternal power; separation of power and property

Power, Susan, 139-140n

productive forces, 15, 144

property, 2, 43, 67, 69, 72, 77, 82; in Filmer, its origin in paternal power, 43-44; and ruler-subject relationship, 44; and master-servant relationship, 44; and his contemporary royalists, 44-45; in Locke, man as God's property, 69,

74, 75, 81; as natural right, 45; its origin in labor, inheritance and charity 45; common, 45; private, 45; and inclusive and exclusive rights, 45-46; in natural and positive community, 47; and appropriation, 46-49, 51, 54; and labor, 47-49; of land, 47-48; and the (Lockean) proviso, 48; and consent, 48-49; and the robbery argument, 48-49; and inheritance, 49; and charity, 49; and absolute property, 56; and ruler-subject relationship, 50; and master-servant relationship, 50-53; and social division of labor, 50-53; and alienation of labor, 50-53; in civil society, 54-56; and resistance, 134-136; *see* also Marxism; separation of power and property

Prynne, William, 21n

Public good, *see* **common good**

Pufendorf, Samuel, 30, 38n, 47, 59-60n, 85, 101n

Ramsey, I.T., 37n

Rau, Zbigniew, 145n

Rawls, John, 15, 18, 19

reductionism, 9, 10, 11

Rea, Bruno, 65n

Reiss, Hans, 23n

religious fundamentalism, 3

resistance, 2, 3, 10, 55, 124, 144; absent in Filmer, 124-128; in Locke, 128-138; circumstances of, 128-130; possibility of, 131-133; as achievable project, 133-134; not a social revolution, 135-138

Ruben, D.H., 22n

Rousseau, 12, 15-18, 22-23n

Russel, Paul, 85, 101n

Ryan, Alan, 65n

Sabine, G.H., 98n

Salamasius, 36n

Schochet, Gordon, 6, 7, 20, 36n, 120n

separation of power and property, 43, 45, 53-57; in the state of nature, 45-53; in civil society, 54-56

separation between right and wrong, right and might, norms and facts, absent in Filmer, 25-28; in Locke, 28-35

separation of legislative and executive, 115

servants, 44, 50, 51, 52

Seliger, Martin, 35, 39n, 41n, 62n, 64n, 99n, 102n, 120-121n, 140n

Shaftesbury, Earl, 1, 22n

Sherington, Robert, 58n

Sherlock, William, 100n

Sidney, Algernon, 23n

Skinner, Quentin, 58n, 140n

slaves, 32, 44, 70, 136; and the prohibition of suicide, 75

Smith, J. A., 98n

social contract, 13, 18, 68, 78, 81-82, 85, 87-88, 134, 137; as foundation of civil society, 69, 76; and the transfer of natural powers, 72; and the end of state of nature, 72; and the origin of political power, 73; and the limits of political power, 74, 76, 78-79

social and political relations, 9-10; made by paternal power, 9-10; man-made, 10

Spelman, John, 23n

spirit of capitalism, 52

society, *see* **civil society**

sovereignty, 8, 106, 113-114, 118; in Filmer, 109; in Locke, 109-112; and Bodin's definition of, 109; and man in the state of nature, 110; and civil society, 111-112; and civil government, 111-112; and responsibility, 110-112

state of nature, 25, 29, 43, 57, 70, 72-73, 75- 77, 82, 87-88, 91, 93, 108-110, 114, 116, 131-133; and the relation between right, might, and power, 29-30; proper, 31-33, 50; natural freedom in, 31-32; natural equality in, 32-33, 50; appropriation in, 48; servant master relationship in, 50; separation of power and property in, 45-53; ordinary, 33-35, 131; as "a state of mediocrity", 33; and two natural powers, 72; and resistance, 135-137

state of war, 30, 32, 124, 135; and resistance, 131-133, 135-136; in the state of nature, 132; in civil society, 132-133

Strauss, Leo, 35, 41n, 98n

Stuarts, 21n, 52, 129

Suarez, 15, 18, 44, 58n, 60n

subjects, 26-27, 44-45, 50, 53, 56-57, 68-70, 76-77, 84-85, 90, 92, 94, 117, 124, 128, 130, 133, 137

superhuman agency, 9-10, 13-14, 16-19, 25-26, 43, 106, 125

Tarkov, Nathan, 141n

Thompson, Martyn, 20, 23n

Tribe, Keith, 63n

trust, trusteeship, 10, 13, 109, 118; as legal metaphor, 112; its moral dimension, 113-114; and the historical experience, 114

Tully, James 1, 4n, 35n, 57, 58-60n, 62-64n, 97n

tyranny, tyrant, 30, 44, 106, 124, 126; and political legitimacy, 82-84; and resistance, 128-130

unity of power and property, 43-44, 51-52, 56

usurpation, usurper, 30; and political legitimacy, 82-84; and resistance, 128-130

Vaughn, C.E., 62n, 98n, 101n

Viner, Jakob, 61n

von Leyden, Wolfgang, 37n, 58n, 96-97n, 100n, 119n, 140n

wage relationship, 51-52, 69, 78, 81

Waldron, Jeremy, 63n

Watkings, J.W.N., 22n

Williams, G.L., 58n

Windstrup, George, 95-96n

Wood, Neil, 40n, 57, 65n, 163n

Wolfe, Don M., 97n

workmanship model, 28, 46,

Yolton, John W., 37n, 60n, 96n

Zaichenko, G.A., 141n